TRANSFORMATION

Lord William Armstrong's Vision
of a Demonstration Centre at Cragend Farm
on his Cragside Estate in Northumberland.

Revolutionizing Agriculture and Industry,
defining the Model Farm Concept.

By Lou Renwick

Published in 2024 by FeedARead.com Publishing

TRANSFORMATION

Lord William Armstrong's Vision
of a Demonstration Centre at Cragend Farm
on his Cragside Estate in Northumberland.

Revolutionizing Agriculture and Industry,
defining the Model Farm Concept.

by Anna-Louise Renwick
2024

Unveiling Cragend:

Ancient Farm remodelled into a Demonstration Centre at Cragside, Northumberland by Lord William Armstrong.

At its core, transformation in engineering refers to the strategic integration of new technologies into traditional engineering practices and processes.

by Anna-Louise Renwick

This book is dedicated to everyone who has helped us find new truths
and re-discover hidden gems.
History is for everyone.
We are the custodians for the future.

Contents

Preface

This research has been collated over the course of more than 12 years and is a first-hand reference for the machinery at Cragend Farm.

Purchased in 2011 from The Armstrong family of Bamburgh by Shaun & Lou Renwick, the farm was derelict, and much of its history forgotten.

Cragend Farm Hydraulic Silo is classed as a Grade II* Listed 'Building at Risk' by Historic England.

The remainder of the outbuildings and houses were suggested to have 'potential' and are not listed.

My suggestion, as the author, is to use the Contents Page if you wish to go straight to the machines, but I felt it my duty to write in and around them, as they are of direct and distinguished relevance to this book, and deserve explanation as does the history of the farm.

Definition: "Silo"

A silo (from Ancient Greek σιρός (sirós) 'pit for holding grain' is a structure for storing bulk materials.

Silos are used in agriculture to store fermented feed known as silage, not to be confused with a grain bin, which is used to store grains.

Using this definition the building should really be 'The Cragend Farm Hydraulic Silos', as there are two bays, but we won't argue too much about that at this point.

Indulge yourself in the background and the history behind their existence.

Chapter 1

A Summary of the wider story of the Cragside Estate

There has been much previously written of The Cragside Estate, and now the lost story of Cragend Farm can now be told too.

The National Trust created an Energy Centre based on the work of William George Armstrong at Cragside [16] in Northumberland in the 1980's.

Professor George Irlam [30] wrote an article about this process is 1988.

Pumphouse Cragside credit Cragend Farm

His paper states that:

'one of the exhibits is a hydraulic engine installed in 1868 to drive pumps that supplied the house with fresh water.
The installation was excavated in 1984 and has now been restored to working order by the British Engineerium'.

This research paper has raised questions about other machinery on the site of the original Cragside Estate, that Jonathan Minns [29] of The British Engineerium [13] saw during his visit to Cragside in 1984-85 when he was investigating the site.

My book is a description of the discovery, conservation and a history of the development of a missing link, the hydraulic machinery at Cragend Farm.

Cragend Farm, dates back to well before the 1300's. It was latterly purchased from The Duke of Northumberland as part of the growing estate of Cragside.

It was then re-designed by Sir William Armstrong of Cragside as a demonstration centre to show off his hydraulic equipment and machinery to dignitaries; it also showed the agricultural labourer of the day that modern machinery could be used to their benefit in terms of labour force, taking the natural resource of water pressure to assist with hard labour.

Although to some labourers it was of concern, in terms of work force numbers, it was plainly obvious that these machines could do the work of many men very easily, and in some instances, work that was impossible without machinery to assist them.

Armstrong was, and still is, thought of as a generous man who was philanthropic to his local communities.

Introduction to Cragend Hill

William George Armstrong (1810-1900) was a prominent Victorian engineer who helped establish Britain's industrial innovations. In a long and varied career his main interests emerged to be the production, use and conservation of energy.

The history behind Cragend Hill in Rothbury North Forest.

Cragend Hill has been here for millennia. It is at the end of the Crags! Hence the name Cragend Farm.

King Edward III was the first monarch to give lands to an individual, and he handed them to Baron Henri de Perci in 1331 which included Cragend Farm, with the lands of Rothbury and Warkworth in Northumberland.

Cragend Farm was leased along with Whitefield Farm (to the north of Cragend Hill) some 1000 acres, as a going concern for centuries from the Duke of Northumberland to tenant farmers.

Armstrong bought Cragend Farm to expand his estate c1870's because he needed water on the east side called The Blackburn, which is the boundary with what was formally The Brinkburn Estate.

He developed the first effective hydraulic systems in the 1840's, made major innovations in armaments manufacture in the 1850's during The Crimean War, and was an early generator and user of electricity in the 1870-1880's.

Cragside, his country residence in Northumberland, was built on Cragend Hill, and was the first private house to be lit by hydroelectric power and the first to be properly fitted with Joseph Swan's incandescent lamps.

Armstrong strongly believed in the need for alternative energy sources and in the 1860's he was outspoken as President of the British

Association for the Advancement of Science on the dangers of over-exploitation of Britain's limited coal reserves.

Aside from concerns about depletion, we now know that the extraction and burning of fossil fuels contribute to environmental problems such as air pollution, water pollution, and the release of greenhouse gases.

The latter is a significant factor in climate change which is a priority problem for us all today.

Cragside has been in the care of The National Trust since 1977, after 2nd Baron Lord Armstrong died in 1972.

Located on Cragend Hill, part of Rothbury North Forest, Cragend Farm was owned by His Grace The Duke of Northumberland, and had been tenanted out for centuries, until Lord Armstrong's tenure when he took it in hand.

However, after his death in 1900 it was tenanted out again to local labourers on site, but remained in the ownership of the Armstrong family.

It was not included in the National Trust transaction in 1977 and finally came up for sale in 2011 from The Armstrong Trust.

It was purchased by Shaun & Lou Renwick who have spent over a decade conserving its heritage and unique history.

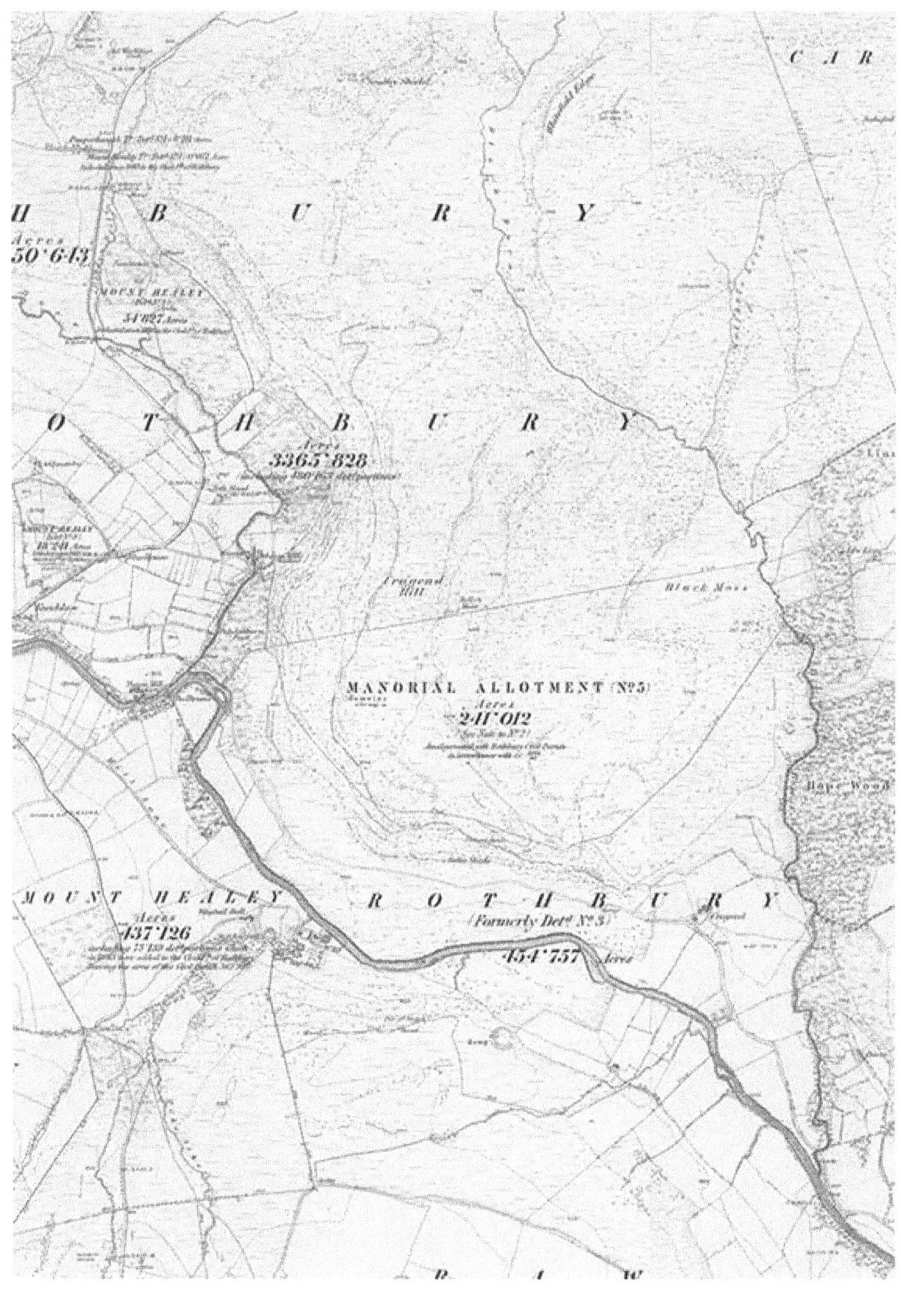

(credit National Library of Scotland OS Map 1864-1865)
Cragend Farm, shown with a Gin-Gan (circular building), was part of a large area on Cragend Hill of some 1000 acres, made up of two farms with Whitefield Farm to the north.

Chapter 2

What was going on in Engineering in the 19th Century

The development of hydraulic engines, hydraulic or water pressure engines arose out of steam technology in the mid-eighteenth century.

As their alternative name implies, they rely on the pressure exerted by a column of water to move a piston in a cylinder. The earliest were similar in design to existing atmospheric steam engines, single acting machines with a counterpoise weight effecting the return stroke.

Armstrong was integral in adding these systems into social environments in Newcastle, with the invention of the water accumulator, and his work on reservoirs, in response to the cholera outbreaks in Newcastle. This put him at the forefront of such engineering work.

At this time, hydraulic engines provided more power than steam engines of similar size and their robustness and reliability made them cheaper to operate and maintain.

Moreover, they were versatile. These advantages led to an enormous increase in their use up to the mid-nineteenth century, with engineers like William Fairbairn, John Darlington and William Armstrong involved in their design and construction.

Armstrong's interest began to grow in the 1840's, after years of working as a lawyer in London. His recreation time was taken up working with Henry Watson [12], who helped him with the development of the hydraulic dockyard equipment that enabled him to start his famous engineering business at Elswick in 1847.

Water pressure engines were a logical extension of his work and he developed machines of increasing sophistication, culminating in multi-cylinder, double-acting devices providing rotary motion for a variety of mining duties.

The Armstrong designs may well represent the peak of hydraulic engine technology for few real improvements were made thereafter and to this day many hydraulic engineering manufacturers continue to use the same principles such as Gilkes Ltd, in Kendal, Lancashire who are now a worldwide supplier of turbines.

Interest in the machines decreased towards the end of the 19th century as steam technology improved again and the railways reduced the cost of transporting coal.

"Trio" Fisher Renwick Screw Steamer 1887 – 1907
c. Cragend Farm

Hydraulic engines had certain insurmountable problems.

They were subject to interruption by frost * and drought and they consumed large volumes of water, which also created an exhaust problem in underground installations.

In addition, the bulk required to withstand their operating conditions meant that they were costly to build and install, perhaps half as much again as the equivalent steam engine by the 20th century.

However, as engineering has improved and green energy has been more relevant, it is notable that in less than 150 years, the technology that Armstrong developed is back in use as a choice for modern installations. [Edradynate hydropower system in Aberfeldy, Scotland as an example, plus any number of Gilkes others, such as the Falkland Islands project.]

*It is notable that Armstrong's machines at Cragside Estate and Cragend Farm are underground and /or within large stone buildings to avoid frost.

The Armstrong Lakes

Lord Armstrong dammed the Debdon Burn to create Tumbleton Lake to safeguard water supplies in 1866 and then again with Debdon Lake in 1870 further up the burn as a holding tank.

Drought [3] [4] caused a water shortage at Cragside later that decade and so he added the Blackburn Lake circa.1870 and Nelly Moss Lakes in 1884-5 [32 pg 116].

The importance of the Blackburn is vital to Armstrong's plan.

It is the sole source of the water for all the top three lakes.

Water was fed from the Blackburn into the Nelly Moss lakes by a 'flume' or aqueduct, it was also supplied water for The Blackburn Lake built as a reservoir solely to power the hydraulics at Cragend Farm.

Dates are sketchy, but it suggests that the droughts circa 1868-1869 rather abruptly changed the way Armstrong was going to source his water from his 1863 original plans to generate power and electricity.

It may explain the large date gap in the purchases in his turbines.

No 395 was purchased from Williamson Brothers (later Gilbert Gilkes) circa 1866 and then no others until No 428 in 1881. Gilkes records indicate that he bought nine turbines in total.

According to Prof. Irlam, Armstrong had originally arranged for the 35 foot (10.7 m) head of water, created to power a hydraulic engine installed at the base of the dam in 1868 in what is now called Tumbleton Pump House.

The engine drove pumps which delivered spring water from a header tank on the roof of the Pump House to a reservoir set into the hillside 150 feet (45.7 m) above. From here it was distributed throughout the main house for domestic purposes. It may also have provided water to power hydraulic lifts, a Whitelaw turbine (recently restored) [1-2] to turn a spit in the kitchen, as yet unproven but written about.

Horizontal Hydraulic lift (jigger) at Cragside to power the elevator.
Credit Cragend Farm.

The two Nelly Moss Lakes and Blackburn Burn Lake/reservoir were created circa 1870-1885 because of the drought difficulties. Armstrong did not want to run out of water again, and it was known that The Blackburn had never run completely dry from its source up on the hill high on Cragend Hill.

The Blackburn runs from the top of the moor down to its exit into The River Coquet and Armstrong re-directed its flow for a number of uses.

Aqueduct at Cragside called the 'Flume'. Credit Cragend Farm.

Chapter 3
The Blackburn Lake

The Blackburn Lake had pipes and a tank that fed into Cragend Farm to give higher drop (200ft) to supply the turbine for the hydro power for the farm.

Blackburn Lake and Boathouse Cragside 2024 credit Cragend Farm.

The Blackburn Lake was drained after a flood that burst the banks of all the Cragside reservoirs in 1927. Tumbleton and Debdon dams were damaged and had to be repaired.

The Blackburn Lake was seemingly blamed for the majority of the damage to The Coquet River due to its size, some 15 acres, and so was hastily drained, although it would appear that none of these lakes are near enough to Rothbury to impact the flooding, and that the Coplish Burn was the main culprit of flooding in Rothbury.

See J. Benn Reservoir article Page 116 and Milky Story Page 124

To this end, the machinery at Cragend Farm can never work again under water power despite being linked to the lake by pipework that still occasionally holds excess water.

This would have been very detrimental to Cragend Farm if they were still using the hydraulic machinery at that point. There is a case to be made that No 490 was as there is a repair bill from Gilkes in 1915.

Chapter 4

The Pumphouse at Cragside

Prof. Irlam only concentrated his paper on the Pumphouse, as for many years this Tumbleton installation was incorrectly called a hydraulic ram.

His research clarified that in fact it was a horizontal, double-acting, reciprocating hydraulic engine, driving an opposing pair of positive displacement plunger pumps.

Historic England Listing
List Entry Name [14] : TUMBLETON RAM HOUSE ON WEST OF DEBDON BURN AT FOOT OF TUMBELTON DAM
Grade: II
List Entry Number: 1042035
Date first listed: 24-Aug-1987

The Cragside Pumphouse. Credit Cragend Farm.

Chapter 5

Cragside
Historic England Listing:
Cragside House is Grade: I
List Entry Number: 1042076
Date first listed: 20-Oct-1953

Cragside was one of the earliest houses to be listed in Britain.

It was the first private house in the world to be lit by electric light (and with hydraulic water powered electricity).

Cragside Estate c. Cragend Farm.

The listing of buildings of special architectural or historical interest was established in the Town and Country Planning Acts of 1944 and 1947. The basis for the first listing survey was the heroic war-time lists, known as 'Salvage Lists'.

In 1971, when advising the National Trust on the most important Victorian houses to be preserved for the nation in the event of their sale, Mark Girouard had identified Cragside as a top priority. A major campaign saw the house and grounds finally acquired by the National Trust in 1977, with the aid of a grant from the National Land Fund, in lieu of death duties.

At that point the whole estate was split up by priority, with the machinery taking second place to the fabric of the main house, explaining why there are missing pieces to this massive jigsaw puzzle of story.

This book now furthers Minn's work and Irlam's earlier research paper, adding historic and factual research to the Cragside Estate story, with the three large pieces of machinery that still stand insitu at Cragend Farm.

They were forgotten and also inaccessible at the time of Minn's report.

Chapter 6

The Powerhouse

BURNFOOT POWER HOUSE, 70 METRES NORTH OF BURNFOOT
LODGE
List Entry Number: 1042071
Heritage Category: Listing Grade: II*

Despite being on the Cragside Estate, The Powerhouse was one of a few remaining historical engineering pieces listed much later, in 1987. This also applied to a number of other machines and areas in and around the Cragside Estate that Armstrong had installed.

The Powerhouse – sited as the place where electricity was generated to power Cragside with a turbine driven by water.

It is now also the home of several other disused turbines, once installed by Armstrong on farms in the area.

The Cragend Farm
Armstrong Machinery

[reference 18]

Chapter 7

No 490 Thomson turbine manufactured by Gilbert Gilkes & Sons (late Williamsons Bros).

The statistics:
30 H.P.
1300 rpm
20 kwh
112 cbftm
190 ft head of water
Vertical Drive shaft
Vortex
Variable Guide Veins

No 490 Thomson turbine with Henry Watson valve [12] and 30 H.P. was manufactured by Gilbert Gilkes (formerly Williamson Brothers) and installed using Armstrong hydraulic pipework.

No 490 Cragend Farm 2010

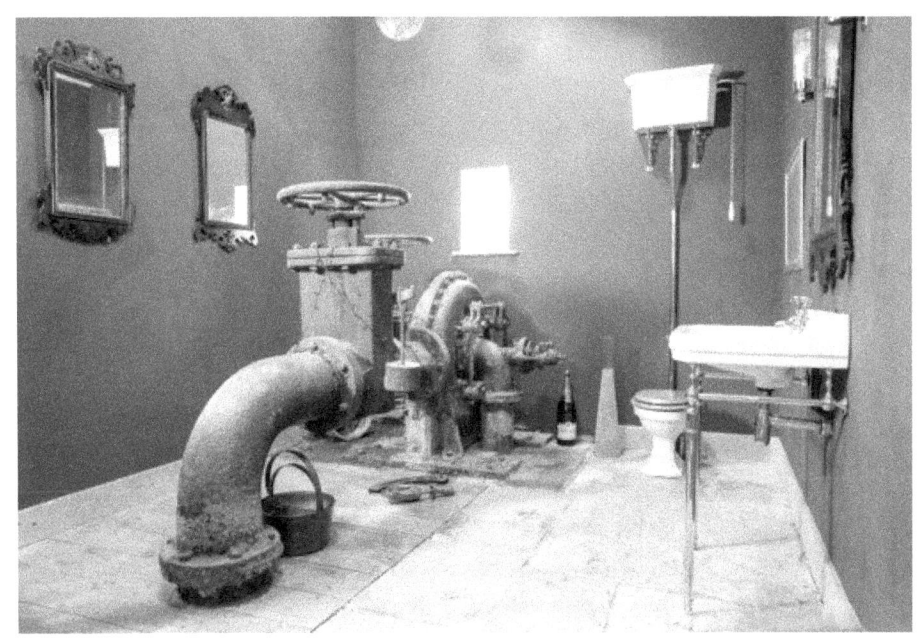

No 490 Cragend Farm 2024

Located in The Turbine Room at Cragend Farm, this Thomson turbine [5] was ordered on August 31st 1883 by Sir William Armstrong (* note not a Lord as yet) and made by Gilbert Gilkes [6] Canal Works, Kendal, Lancashire.

It replaced a gin-gan driven by horses that had previously been there as shown by the circular building in the north section of the buildings.

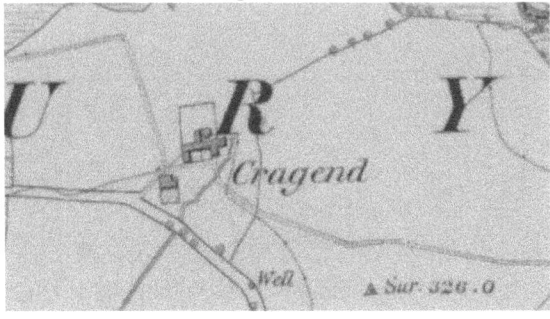

Credit: National Library of Scotland 1864-1865 OS Map.

credit. National Library of Scotland 1894
Map showing all the lakes on the Cragside Estate at their peak with The Blackburn Lake covering 15 acres was the largest of them all.

Armstrong ordered this No 490 turbine from Gilkes along with another similar turbine No 491[15] for a local farm he had also purchased, in nearby Trewitt. Although it was a similar machine, No 491 operated on a much lower head of water with less power.

Cragend Farm No 490 has a 10" inlet and twin 7" outlet, vertical {V} Vortex [31] with moveable guide vanes.

The water flow [Q] through the turbine is 112 cubic feet per minute, equivalent to 698.9 gallons per minute. The theoretical maximum horse power from that flow at a head of 116 feet is 32.24 horse power. However due to the losses in the penstock (due to friction in the penstock pipe when carrying the flow of 116 cubic feet per minute which results in a small reduction of the available head of water at the turbine) and also the fact that the turbine is not able to convert all the energy available from the flow and head of water into power at the shaft means that the factor 0.93 per unit (93%) has to be applied in order to deduce the actual power the turbine will produce. It operates from 190 ft head of water from Blackburn Reservoir/Lake at 1300 rpm.

The Vortex had the great advantage that it could work on any head of water from 3 to 300 feet, it was relatively small, and had an efficiency of 70% to 75%. If fitted with movable guide blades, it would maintain a reasonable efficiency with a low flow of water.

The moveable guide blades helped efficiency and the regulators would be for the pressure prior to the waters entrance into the turbine.

All the remaining metal work relating to the water pipes are from Armstrong's Elswick works with some imprinted 'Newcastle'.

It has a 'Henry Watson' imprinted [12] 'valve' that connects the power source from the turbine to the Silo and would have been added as part of the expansion of work continuing during 1884.

It is unclear if that was always the intention, and the additional pipework suggests that even if always meant the 'plumbing' was added to, as any extension would be.

No 490 powered threshing, awning, milling, rolling and grinding machines in the barns upstairs, next door in The Machine Room, and Threshing Barn.

It had a flywheel to release excess energy if other areas were not in use.

New Information uncovered since 2011

Until recently, it was unclear about the water source entry areas, but we now know that No 490 also powered No 1306 Hydraulic Hoist (previously called a Jigger or Jig) ordered in 18th August 1884 and No 630 Thomson turbine ordered in September 1st 1887 from Gilkes, both located in The Cragend Farm Hydraulic Silo.

Credit: Gilkes Museum, Kendal, Lancs.
No 490 bought by Sir W G Armstrong 30 H.P.

The headings are from left to right on the Gilkes record book:
No = serial number
HP = horsepower
F = Fall … the head of water coming into the turbine.
Name = client or sometimes the factor/agent of an estate
Position = vertically [V] or horizontally [H] arrangement
Blades = Mov indicates movable guide vanes Fixed indicated fixed guide vanes [most were movable]
Q = water flow rate probably cu ft / min
Supply = Diameter of supply [inlet pipe]
Suction = diameter of outlet pipe… referred to as suction because the "draft tube" below a turbine creates suction and effectively increases the operating head which is a combination of the fall plus the suction of the draft tube.

Electricity generation possibilities:

No 490 had enough power to generate 20kw of electrical power and it had been suggested that it was meant to be attached to a dynamo in order to do so.

Professor J. Wrightson, wrote in the Newcastle Daily Journal January 21 1887 [17] about this, with the later building of the Cragend Farm Hydraulic Silo:

"...As indicating the versatility of Sir Williams genius, it may be well to remark that by a combination of hydraulics and electricity it is his intention to cultivate all his arable land by means of a fixed electrical engine charged by means of revolving magnets actuated by waterpower. This we saw in progress of erection and so far, advanced was it that before the 'Royal' visits Newcastle it may be in the active operation veritably ploughing the land by means of the electric spark."

[32] The Diss Express Newspaper (Norfolk) states that a Royal visit to the farm was arranged in 1884, Prince and Princess of Wales, (King Edward VII and Queen Alexandra) and The Newcastle Courant in 1888 by Princess Louisa and her husband The Duke of Argyll.

These visits by the great and the good were very divisive. It was incredible new technology and everyone who was anyone wanted to see it in action, and buy it for their estates.

It is notable that both The Duke of Devonshire and the Duke of Northumberland, to name but a few, both bought Gilkes turbines for their estates, after the Cragend Farm model was installed and exhibited.

Pipework Details.

The Blackburn Lake hillside reservoir is designed to encourage the settling of solid material that may have been carried over from the burn.

Water enters the reservoir tangentially so that a whirlpool effect is created. Centrifugal force causes particles to migrate to the side where they lose kinetic energy and sink to the bottom. Clear water for use is drawn from the top of the tank that is still located on the Cragside Estate above the farm located in woodland between the reservoir and the farm (see OS map 1898).

There is a metal pipe that runs through the field above the farm from the tank to the entry point of the No 490 turbine and runs underneath the wooden cow 'huts' (shed/byres) and cobbled pathway which we must assume were built after the pipework was laid c1883.

Most remarkable about this re-modelling of Cragend Farm, is the planning and forethought that went into making this all possible. Any builder will tell you that the 'first fix' is integral to any build and the excavations, plumbing plus additional stonework to buildings was considerable.

The archaeological report of 2012 [10] records the different stages that the farm buildings went through, and this in an unexhaustive area, as we continue to find new information about the site.

"Below floor level the associated pipework for the turbine shows the main 10 inch inlet pipe, twin outlet pipes, which rejoin into one and travel to the main drain, as well as a bypass pipe with a gate valve allowing a flow of water to bypass the turbine altogether, allowing maintenance to be carried out on all elements of the turbine and pipework above that point. The general design of the turbine would indicate it is <u>a Francis</u> type turbine, possibly Gilkes No 490".
ARS report on Cragend Farm 2012

A correction of this and other research can now be confirmed with documentation in terms of their records, books and letters from Gilkes that the Cragend Farm turbines are not a Francis/Turgo/Pelton.

The first Pelton turbine was produced by Gilkes at No 921, and Francis turbine in 1920, so therefore both Cragend turbines are definitely Thomson turbines, engineered by and as confirmed by Gilkes today.

Gilkes Order Book for No 490
Credit Gilkes Museum, Kendal

There is some argument about whether 'all' turbines are tangential which may also raise an eyebrow.

It would be accurate to say that they can only work if they are tangent. The water has to enter at a certain angle to move the blades.

The additional buildings of 'The Turbine Room' and 'The Machine Room' were built above a stone encased trap, replacing a Gin-Gan, show in OS map 1864.

Cattle huts (byres) and cobbles & The Machine Room 2024 (once the gin-gan)

It housed the water pipework, and extended away south from No 490 underground and the pipe never raised above ground again, as it snaked its way to a soak away drain located approx. 50m from the turbine.

It turns sharp left towards another building on the farm, specifically built by Lord Armstrong, and unlike those where he reconstructed ancient buildings to build these machine rooms, this is a brand-new building – a demonstration centre.

ORDER NO. 490 - AUGUST 1881
30 HP 190 FT. 7 CFS   1300 RPM
FOR BURNFOOT POWER HOUSE
INCLUDING SUNDRIES ORDERED MARCH 1885
AND TURBINE WHEEL REPAIRED MAY 1913

63.

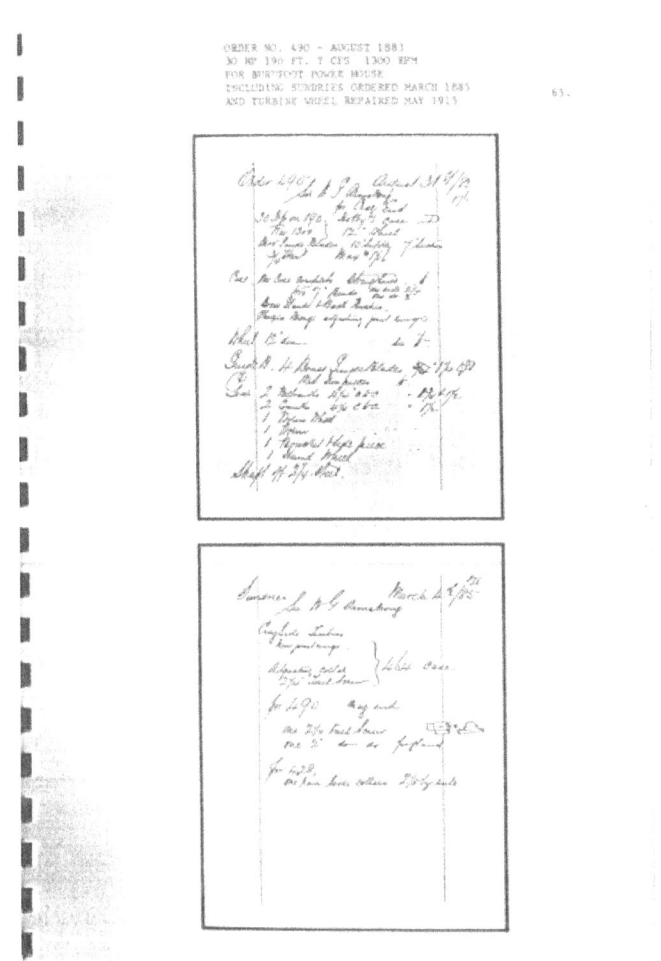

No 490 Order details.
Reproduced with permission of National Trust from
the Cragside archive.

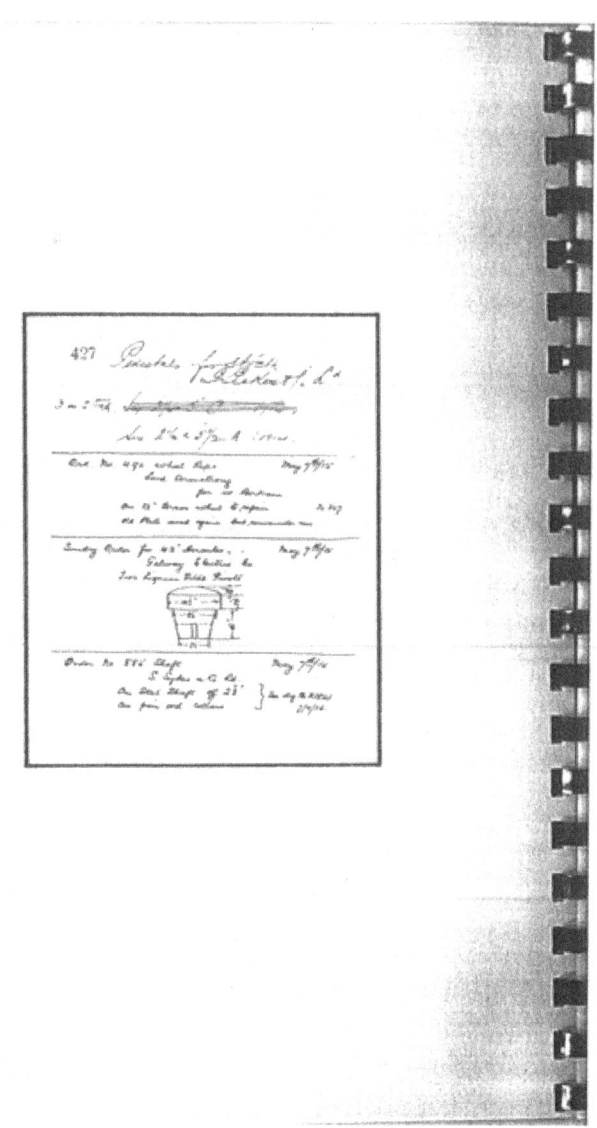

Details of repairs to no 490 in 1915.
Reproduced with permission of National Trust
from the Cragside archive.

Details from the letter to Armstrong from Gilkes
Tyne and Wear Archives

Order 490   August 31st /83 [1883]

        Sir William Armstrong

For Crag End

30 HP on 190 [ft]   Hobbys case D
Rev 1300   12 inch wheel

Mov [movable] guide blades 10 inch supply 7 inch suction
¾ [of an hour?} d max on 1& 1/16

Case: 1 case complete strengthened to from 7 inch bands one side 2
¼ in one side 2 in
brass blades back bushes
Phosphor Bronze adjusting joint hinges

Wheel 12 inch diameter
?See } Brackets[b/gudgets] 4 brass guide blades [¾ crossed out] 1 ¼
?
Gear 2 Bellrails? for 4 ¼   C to C cwc?   2 ¾ and 1 ½
2 Cranks 4 ¼
1 ??? orne wheel
1 ???
1 parallel ? bracket side piece?
1 hand wheel
Shaft off 2 ¼ steel

For 490 Cragend (1883)
1 ¼ Fuel? Tail screw
1 2 inch fuel? ditto tail crew for gland

No 490 31/08/1883 W G Armstrong for Crag End

30hp on 190 Hobbys case D
Rw 1300 (revs per min?) 12" qwheel
Mov Guide Blades 10 inch supply 7 inch suction
¾)?) Max ??
? Bronze adjusting joint nearings
Wheel 12" diam

1915 May 7th (to 307)
490 wheel repair
Lord Armstrong
Per w. Bertram
Onw 12" brass wheel to repair
Old plate used again but remainder new.

Chapter 8

The Cragend Farm Hydraulic Silo

Historic England listing:
Listed Building Grade: II*
List Entry Number: 1153196
Date first listed: 24-Aug-1987
List Entry Name: Cragend Farm Hydraulic Silo
Statutory Address: Hydraulic silo building 45 metres east of Cragend
Farmhouse, Rothbury, NE65 7XN

Statistics
1 ton hydraulic hoist

3 H.P. Gilkes turbine
4 " inlet pipe
200 ft head of water

36 1 ton weights

The Cragend Farm Hydraulic Silo was built of stone on ground level and rises high above the other buildings, banked up by more stone and earth on all sides.

The basement level is completely covered so as to give the impression of being underground.

The pipe from No 490 enters The Silo on the south side at the basement level. There are no other pipes into this building.

There is an outlet pipe that is horizontal to the inlet pipe and that leads to soak away.

There are also some soak away areas linked to rain water goods from gutters and downpipes on both sides of the silo bays.

Inside the central tower of this building is No 1306 Hydraulic hoist [22] made by Armstrong, with a Henry Watson valve and the later, additional, unique No 630 Thomson turbine made by Gilkes, all installed using Armstrong hydraulic pipework.

The listing is not specific about the machinery.

No 1306 Hydraulic Hoist

A technical drawing of the building and the hoist was found in 2023 by Lou Renwick in a search of The Tyne and Wear Archives [3] [19] [20] and gives much clearer insight into the original creation and what mechanisms were in place.

Tyne & Wear Archives Reading Room

This diagram is waxed linen and comes from the Armstrong-Vickers archives; it would have been the technical drawing for the engineering side of construction of the building.

The diagram is labelled:
Sir W. G. Armstrong Cragside 1 Ton Hoist
This gives some idea of date as he was not made a Lord until 1887.

The archaeologists had suspected that the building was built in sections, and the diagram shows that the tower [25] and east bay were built first. The second bay must have been added later once they knew that the building operated sufficiently.

It is worth mentioning that the building is more balanced with both silo bays, and it is arguable that it was always his intention to have two bays, and may have been an homage to the Border Reivers as he was an Armstrong.

The dates on the drawing are vitally important.

The notation 'Erecting plan sent 26/8/84' gives us some idea that the building work was happening in 1884 which is over a decade earlier than first thought by Historic England who had dated it c1895.

This has now been amended on the Historic England listing due to this document.

There are three drawings on the diagram; one showing an overhead view, one a view from the east and one a view from the west.

These drawings are coloured in parts and covered in notations relating to all the areas required to make the building an engineering success.

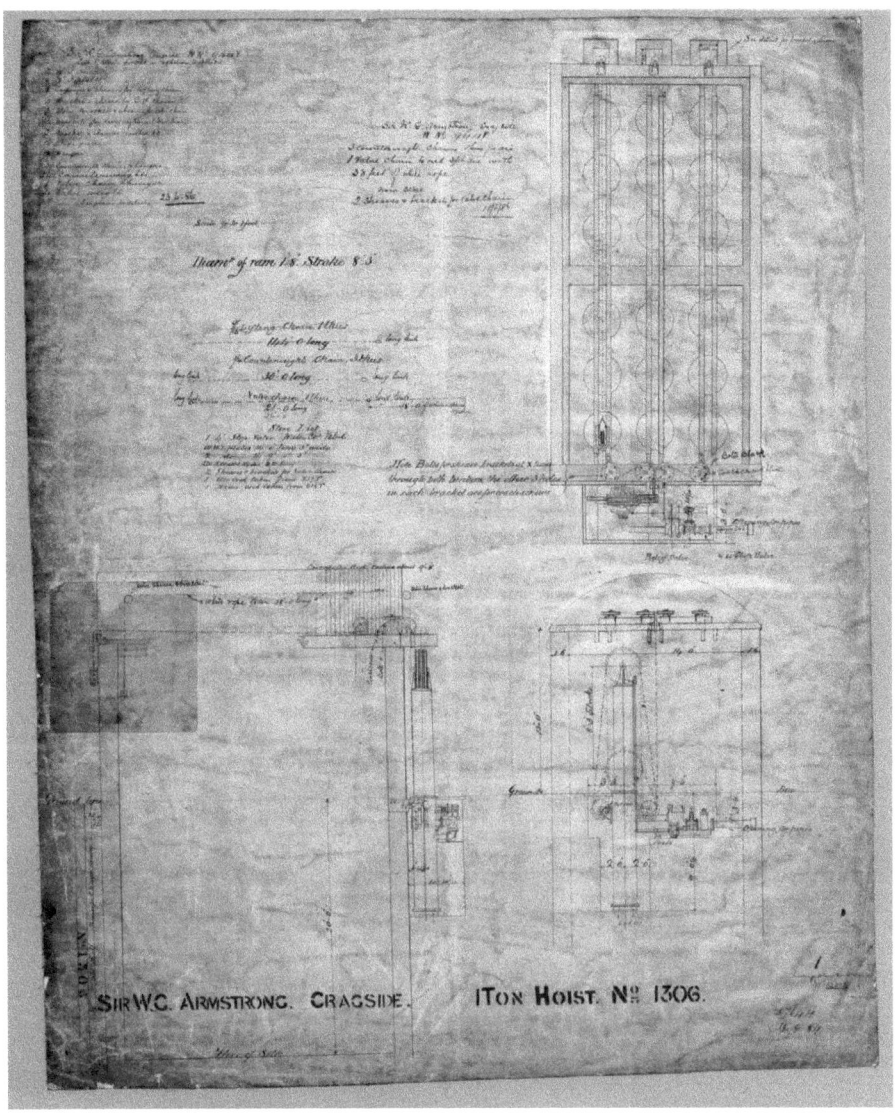

DS.VA/5/PL/11/8, plan no. 1306

Credit Tyne & Wear Archives (Discovery Museum).
No 1306 Sir W G Armstrong 1 Ton Hoist at Cragend Farm

Chapter 9

The Three Diagrams on the Technical drawing explained.

The overhead view:

This dissection of the building is an overhead view and gives us a clear guide to the massive weights that are located in the base of the silo bay and the girders that run in the roof above them. Also, the stone trap at the east end for chains and extra weights.

The weights are 2 feet high and 4 feet in diameter. Based on them being cut from solid stone they are approximately 1 ton weight each. Each has a metal ring on the top. There are no notations about them on the diagram however agricultural journalist Wrightson notes: "18 massive cheese shaped weights all held securely by iron rings and clamps" and they "hang like church bells when elevated".

There is also a detailed drawing of the hoist from above showing the inlet and outlet pipes.

This information confirms the power is coming from water entering the building from the south side of the building. It gives information on pulleys (sheaves), brackets, chains, coach screws, black bolts required.

There are also some notes:

Notes on the opening for pipes, the relief valve and 4 stop valves:

Note Bolts for sheave brackets at X pass
Through both timbers the other 3 holes
In each bracket are for coach screws.

The North East View:

This diagram shows the corrugated sections of roof which are very clearly drawn out and marked:

Corrugated roof radius about 9'-8''
Store Sheave bracket
White rope 5/8" diameter Rope 38'-0" long
Coach screw
Bolt

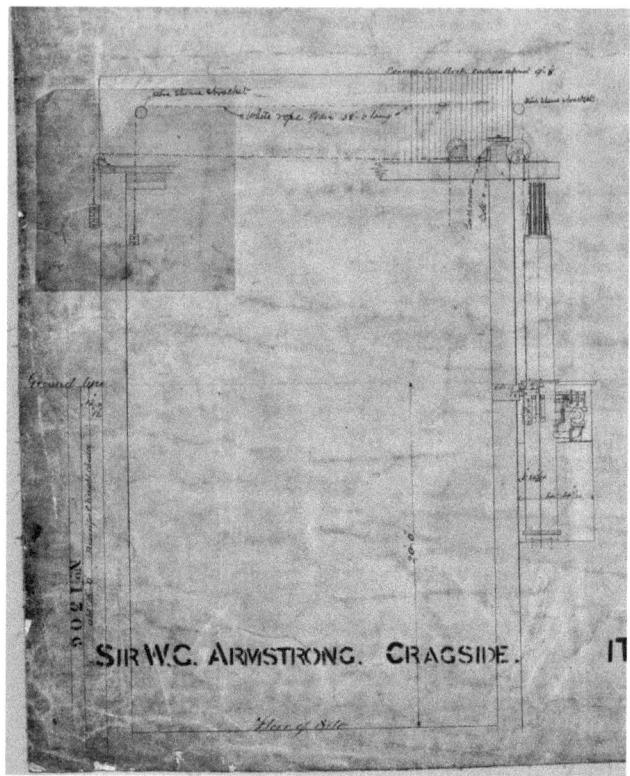

The east end chamber is clearly visible as on the overhead view.

This concludes the fact that it was not an add-on but an original part of the design.

This note to the right of the diagram indicates the length of chain required at the east side of the building for the depth of these three chambers:

16'- 0" Recess for C Weight chain

The chambers are noted as being 12" wide.

From the *Floor of the Silo* to the top is labelled as 20'-0"

On the left of the diagram are a number of notes about the hoist.

The pit for the hoist is shown as 4'- 4¼'' wide with the chain sitting at 1'- 4¼'' from the wall vertically.

At the point where the main wheels of the hoist are positioned are some smaller notations 3'-0'' x 1'-0'' [1-8] [1 2" ¼ ?]
It should be noted that the floor of the Silo is not the same as the floor level of the hoist pit

The West View:

This diagram shows the engine tower section that houses the hoist.

There is a clear line marked 'Ground Line' that cuts this diagram in to two sections. Below that line is marked 'Opening for pipes' with a depth of 3'-6" marked below the line which tells us how deep down the pipes are located.

[These pipes have been detected using a metal detector for the most part to check they are there with a few areas of excavation having been done at the entry point of No 490 and below the Silo]

The hoist is stated as being grounded/stabilised 9'-0 ½'' below the ? is ground level.

The pit that the hoist is positioned in is **4'- 0 x 3'- 0 x 9'- 0**
The central line of the hoist is positioned at equal distance of 2'-0'' of this 4' pit.

It can be suggested that this pit may have had wooden boards over the space so that workers could walk on them and adjust the machinery however the large length of chain may have been rested in the pit or on the floor of the building.

 The left hand wheel (north) of the hoist is labelled **'Fast End'.**

The dimensions extend to 3'- 3" at the left small wheel level to the centre point of the large wheel, and with the remaining area being stated as 7'- 6"

Notation: **8'- 3" Stroke is from the centre of the larger main wheel to its highest centre point, with the width overall being 14'-0" plus 1'-6' either side for the stone walls.**

Notation: **13' height from the girders in the roof to the base Ground Level.**

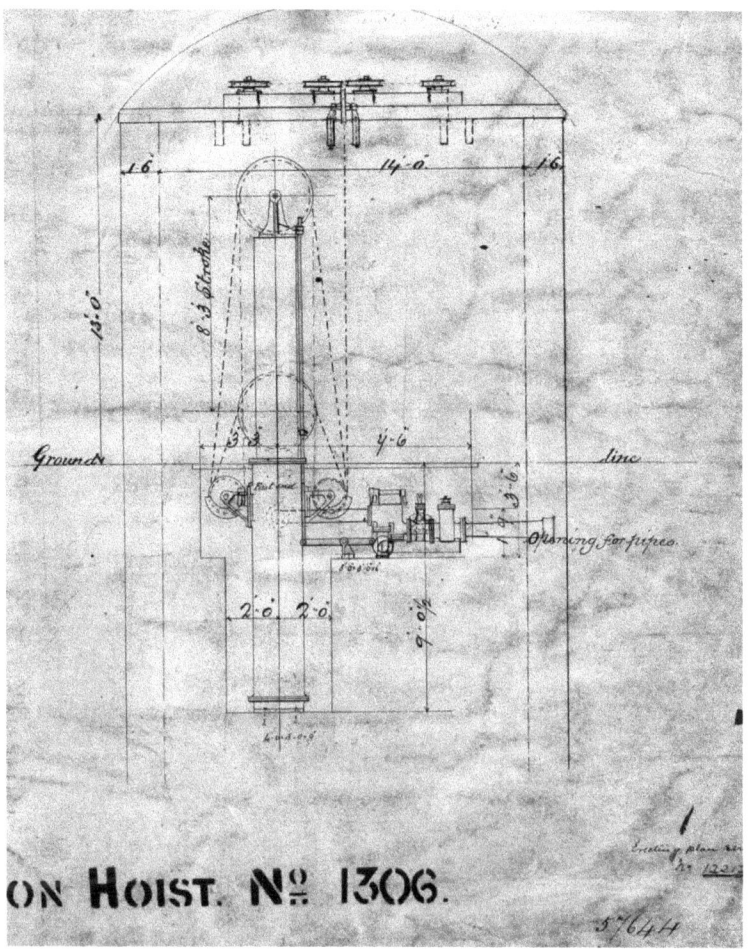

ON HOIST. No 1306.

57644

Below this diagram is stated:

Erection plans sent 26.08.84 Number 12212

57644 [this is perhaps a works number based on other documentation researched]
18 8 84 [Date: 18th August 1884]

In the centre of the drawing are more notations which give us other guidance about each drawing.

Diameter of Ram 1'-8" inch stroke 8'-3" inches [51cm diameter 2.5514m stroke]

9/16 lifting chain 1 thus
144'-0 long long link [drawn on line]------------------------
¼ counterweight chain 3 thus
30'-0 long link [drawn on line]------------------------
Valve chain one thus 21'-0 long [drawn on line]----------------------

34'-0 [drawn on line]------------------------

Store list:
1 4" stop valve Water Co valve

~~10 WI plates 14"-0 long 5" wide~~ crossed out
~~2 ditto 14' 9". 5".~~ Crossed out
~~220 screws 3/8 dia. 2 ½ long~~
2 sheaves and brackets for Valve chain
1 air cock taken from 217 T
1 drain cock taken from 218 T

An air cock is a small tap or valve for controlling the entrance or escape of air from a pipe, chamber, etc.

A drain cock is a tap or valve used to regulate or draw off water from the lowest part or a tank. In essence a tap.

There is an added note opposite the overhead diagram on its left:

Sir W. G. Armstrong W number 944V [Works No?]
3 counterweight chains thus ¼ diameter
1 valve chain 2 med ? 3/16 diameter with
38 feet of white rope

From Store
2 sheaves and brackets for valve chain 18/6/86 [18th June 1886]

This is an amendment to the original technical drawing

The top left of the drawing has substantial notations on the extras needed for this task:

Sir W G Armstrong Cragside W.No. 944V
List of details ordered in addition to 1306phase
 Hst [Hoist]
2 W I knees?
6 W I Plates?
3 carriages and sheaves for lifting chain
3 brackets and sheaves for valve chains
36 brackets for carrying stone
2 brackets and sheaves marked AA
18 slide pieces
14? hangers
3 ??counterweights and hangers
24 ?? counterweights
1 valve chain and hanger
4 valve weights

How did The Cragend Farm Hydraulic Silo work?

It is now far easier to explain how this building was intended to work, because of this technical data.

Silage was invented in Germany, using a pickling process. It was already being attempted with some success in Britain, albeit a very labour intensive process.

Armstrong, was well aware of this fact, and saw an opportunity to use his hydraulic engineering processes to demonstrate how even the most labour intensive tasks could be mechanically achieved using water power.

No 1306 Armstrong hydraulic hoist

Phase 1 1884-1885

Silage starts out as grass in the fields which is usually ready in late May. These are fields that haven't been grazed since the winter to allow the grass to grow. It's really important that the grass is cut when it contains its highest nutrient levels which is usually late spring early summer when the weather is sunny and dry.

Silage is thought to have been invented in Germany, lightly based on a sauerkraut recipe in the early 19th century. A French agriculturalist named Auguste Goffart wrote about it in 1877 and its benefits, and ensilage was produced with limited success until the First World War when it stopped being made so extensively until the late 1950's.

The hydraulic hoist is first used to lift the 18 stone weights that sit at the base of the silage bay. Each one was lifted individually and pegged into position on the top girders using a large heavy metal peg. A small boy would climb along the girders to do this 'pegging' balancing some 20 feet above the Silo floor.

Professor Wrightson wrote that the "parallel strong trussed iron girders from each of which like bells in a belfry hang" these stone weights.

Some of the 18 1-ton weights in East Bay

Grass grown in nearby fields was cut and brought by horse drawn cart to the main doors of the Silo building.

The grass would have been cut by hand, using shears, and brushed into the silage bay that was located through door openings on the left and right.

Wrightson notes,

"Five or six men are engaged treading in the green stuff especially taking care that it is tightly packed at the edges next to the cement walls. Finally, it is covered with thick boards…"

The walls are a limecrete render on sandstone walls and would have been quite white until the silage stained it green.

Once the site is prepared, and the grass in place, the Hoist is then employed again to lower the stone weights on to the boards.

Wooden and metal girders with one long metal beam like a RSJ and corrugated curved roof.

It could take several months before the silage was ready to recover.

To remove the silage, the process was done in reverse, with the Hoist being used to lift each one of the weights to the top position hanging from the girders.

At this point, it becomes less clear what would have happened, but the diagram gives us some clues.

The wooden boards would have been removed and the silage dug out using a silage knife cutter. [23]

The silage may have been elevated out of the bay using pulleys and a platform, which is suggested in the diagram notes about all the sheaves and ropes.

First it would have just been taken by cart straight from the Silo, but latterly the silage was then placed in a shute, that led to an add-on cart shed on the north west side of the second Silo bay and then collected in a cart and driven to the cow huts/byres at the rear if the farm, to feed the cattle.

The Ginnell: Cow huts or byres c1988 (page 96)

Chapter 10

Armstrong's Prize Cattle 1873-1908

Armstrong had a 70 head herd of Beef Shorthorns at Cragend Farm from c1873 until they were sold as discovered in this newspaper article.

The Evening Chronicle February 28th 1908 stated, 'On Thursday April 9 1908 the entire herd of purebred shorthorns the property of Lord Armstrong will be offered for sale by auction at Cragend… the history of the herd is interesting …in 1873 'Mr Gow purchased for the late Lord Armstrong two heifers at considerable cost. They were Duchess of Geneva roan, Wild Duchess of Geneva 2nd red and the following year, their sister.'

They lived in the cattle sheds above the barns, and could be seen form the carriage drive.
They were part of his plan to demonstrate how hydraulic water power could be used to assist agriculture… by feeding them on silage made in a Silo.

Armstrong is noted to have made comment, "[he] spoke highly of silage as a food and his men are equally enthusiastic in his praise. The butter retains its summer hue through the depths of winter and the cattle are as fat as butter. The milk resembles cream and the flavour is never affected except beneficially. Lady Armstrong is as much alive to the advantage of ensilage as her husband who avers of others that 1 ½ tons of silage are as good as 1 ton of hay."

Cragside paintings of Beef Shorthorns: Roan, red and white shorthorns, with white shorthorns being the only ones to breed with a Galloway to breed a Blue-grey for beef sales

Cragend Rare Breed Whitebred Shorthorn Cattle: Cragend Farm 2024

Another article taken from The Morning Post September 24th 1888 states:

"The shorthorns are kept on the home farm at Cragend but on a distant part of the estate there are a few Kyloes [West Highland Cattle] and Galloways, the former being bought for bought in for grazing purposes, and the latter being crossed with Shorthorn bulls for the production of the now popular blue-greys. The dairy in which lady Armstrong takes great interest is attached to the house and is fitted with centrifugal separator and churn both worked by a turbine the milk being the produce of a small herd of Jerseys which appear to thrive well in their northerly and mountainous surroundings."

As suggested in the article, the white bulls were used to sire calves with a Galloway cow to make a Blue-Grey, which still happens today.

Phase 2 1885-1887

No 630

By 1884 there was plenty of correspondence between the engineers as to how to progress this 'demonstration centre' farm and despite only very few letters surviving, it creates a detailed picture of all that was being discussed on both sides.

Letter from Gilkes to Armstrong regarding the sale of equipment:

3rd March 1884 (Letter from Gilkes to Armstrong)

Dear Sir

We are duly in receipt of your valued enquiry of the 1st ?first ?date? and in the course of a post or two we shall send you full particulars as to the machine we recommend <u>for chopping green forage for ensilage</u>.

We should judge that it will require 4 to 6 horsepower to drive it. Before sending you a tracing of a reaction wheel we venture to enclose with this a tracing of a tangent turbine which has been significantly at work for many years yielding 4 HP. For your purpose it would be necessary to have the adjusting nozzle of which we also enclose a tracing. The diameter of the wheel in your case would be 16 inches and the power could be regulated by the adjustable nozzle from half a horse however to 6 or 7 HP. We should propose to extend the spindle of the turbine until it came ? immediately below the chaff cutter and ran? direct from it; the speed of the horizontal spindle being from 700 to 800 revolutions per minute.

Taking into consideration the immediate bevel? gearing on the upright spindle which it would necessitate, the further loss of forward power in the water junction of a re-action wheel we have no hesitation in stating it to be our belief that the tangent turbine proposed will be more economical of water and more readily adjustable than the re-action wheel.

We can make one and will do so with pleasure if you wish it, but having just taken one out on account of its inefficiency the trouble it gave, we should much rather make a tangent turbine for you. The price of a tangent turbine made after the style of the tracing enclosed would be 27 pounds 15 shillings

Yours respectfully Gilbert Gilkes

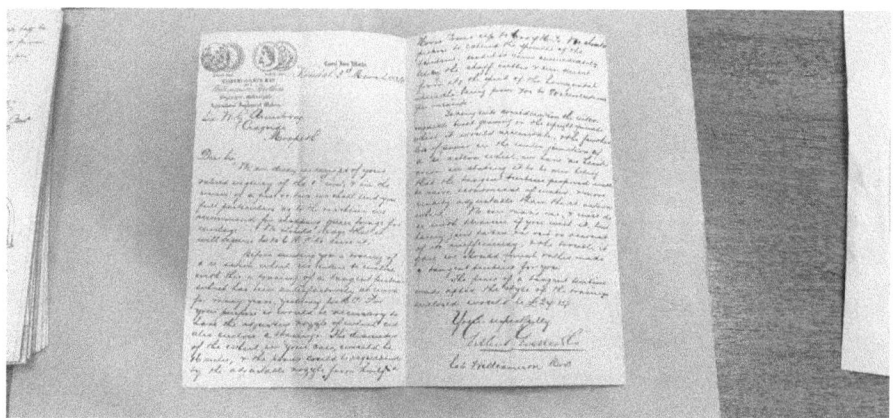

Tyne & Wear Archives credit

The result was the order placed for 3 HP Thomson turbine as described by Tom Hay in Northern Mills Magazine some decades later, which has since been used as a research point that required some clarity.

Nº	HP	F	NAME	P	?73	PATTERN	Q	Supply	Just
620	30	22	Renishaw Kingf.	V		N. case 273	963	x	18
621	30	22	Renishaw Kingf.	V		N. case 273	963		18
622	30	40	Leighycroft Foundry Co	V	M	R. case	230	20	14
623	80	23	Government N.W.	V	M	hwd	2510	Rustamp	4
624	37	28	Howard Farrar &	V	M	N. case	933	29	20
625	5	80	Alexander & Duncan	V	M	X. case	44	7	5
626	80	42	Fairbrook Lim &	V	M	A.N. case	1345	30	20
627	45	33	Howard Farrar &	V	M	O. case	965	26	18
628	60	36	A. Laurette	V	M	N. Vertical	1176	30	21
629	10	38	N. Middleton	V	M	V. case	190	12	8
630	3	200	Lord Armstrong	V	M	new	42		
631	25	90	N. Lloyd	V	M	U.	196	14	10
632	6¾	14½	R. Courage	V	M	R.	328	16	11
633	33	30	Sandisgrth & Co	V	M	P.	777	25	16
634	45	26	A. E. Read	V	M	A.N	1222	33	21
36	4	34	Alexander & Duncan	V	M	W. Nobly	83	9	6
635	22	12	J.C. Satchem	V	M	A.N. super	1295	33	20
637	12	20	A. Mallis	V	M	R. case	430	18	14
638	100	47	N. Shaw & Sons	V	M	A.N. case M	1303	36	22
639	1⁹⁸⁄₁₀₀	7	Northwich Union Rural	H	M	T. case	200	14	0
640	20	20	E. Knowles	V	M	A case	706	24	16

No 630 Turbine Courtesy Gilkes Museum Kendal.

No 630 Gilkes Thomson turbine. c Cragend Farm 2024

Is it a tangent?
Is it a reaction?
What did Armstrong choose?
Did Armstrong follow Gilkes recommendations?

In 1886 further adjustments were made to the building and machinery as per the technical diagram.

Armstrong discussed with Gilkes a small turbine to operate a chaff-cutter inside the Silo. It was an attempt to ease the work of the men further by reducing the need for cutting the grass by hand with shears.

We may conclude that Armstrong got his way and this is an Armstrong special, rather than the 4 H.P. that Gilkes suggested, as it is a 3 H.P. Thomson turbine.

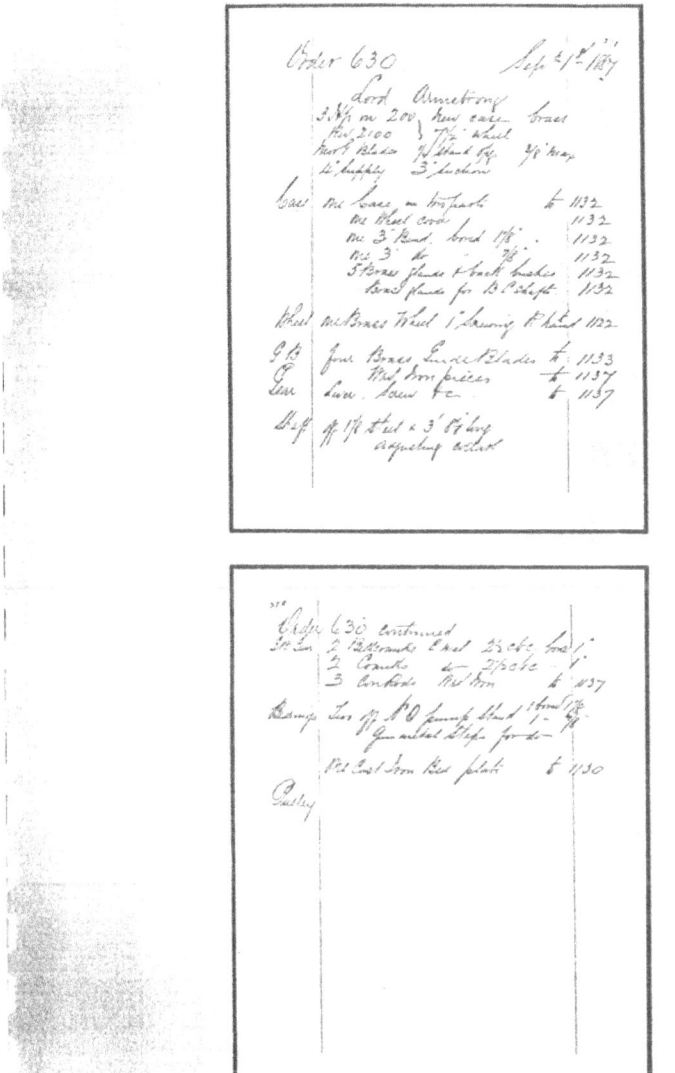

credit. National Trust Archives Cragside.
Details referencing No 630 at Cragend Farm.

Referred to by Tom Hay [8] as a "Tangent turbine" and referenced in Encyclopaedia Britannica, 1893, as "Professor James Thomson's inward flow or vortex turbine has been selected as the type of reaction turbines."

Reaction turbines are the turbines that use the pressure as well as the velocity of the moving water to rotate.

Reaction turbines are placed in the water stream where the water enters the casing tangentially. After rotating the blades, the water axially leaves the casing of the turbine.

Classed at the time as:
 "one of the best even in normal conditions of working, and the mode of regulation introduced is decidedly superior to that in most reaction turbines; it might almost be said to be the only mode of regulation which satisfies the conditions of efficient working, [and it has been adopted in a modified form in the Leffel turbine, which is now largely used in America]. The turbine has suction pipes, which permit the turbine to be placed at any height less than 30 feet above the tail-water level. The water enters the turbine by cast-iron supply pipes at A, and is discharged through two suction pipes S. The water on entering the case distributes itself through a rectangular supply chamber SC, from which it finds its way equally to the four guide-blade passages G. In these passages it acquires a velocity about equal to that due to half the fall, and is directed into the wheel at an angle of about 10 or 12 degrees with the tangent to its circumference. The wheel W receives the water in equal proportions from each guide-blade passage."

See diagram in EB [21]

Restoration/Conservation

Major work started in 2012 with the repair of the Silo slate apex roof and sky lights.

The Turbine Room (Room 1 Q ARS) was excavated, cleaned and new floor boards installed to encase the underfloor pipes.

In 2019 the Silo floors were re-instated and the doors and window repaired. A quoin stone was replaced, saving a door lintel.

In 2022 the east bay was excavated and the 18 one tone weight stones were unearthed.

Currently in phase 3, the work is ongoing.

Chapter 11

H. Pooley & Sons Weigh Machine (OS 1898 W.M.)

A two axel weigh scale plate is located to the south of the main buildings with a small outbuilding that houses the mechanics for the scale including weights, and some graffiti - mathematical calculations on the lime plaster on the interior.

Originally on show at The Great Exhibition 1851, Armstrong purchased three machines. The Cragend Farm machine is the only to survive in its entirety.

Restored in 2014 with a new roof, conserved window and door, the plate and interior mechanics now work.

The weighbridge plate was found under a mass of mud and grass and had been covered up for some time as it is not mentioned in the sale particulars.

This weigh machine (WM) on the OS is on there from 1898 however, it disappears on there from the 1950's.

We decided to renovate it with Roger Kagan and Stephen Lunn's help, and it took 3 years to get the mechanism working. Also, new roof, and a conservation repair to the window and door.

Roger Kagan with Delilah and the weigh machine.

The weighbridge plate was found under a mass of mud and grass and had been covered up for sometime as it is not mentioned in the sale particulars.

We decided to renovate it with my fathers help, and it took 3 years to get the mechanism working. A new roof, and conservation repair.

A Two axle plate made by H. Pooley & Sons c 1860 E.E. No 234 Exhibited at the Great Exhibition in London 1851, as was William Armstrong's Water powered Hoist. They must have met!

69

Shaun Renwick and Roger Kagan replace the weigh plate.

Roger Kagan de-rusting the weigh machine internal mechanism

Conclusion

It is fair to say that the work done by Lord Armstrong from 1863-1900 made a massive impact on The Coquet Valley as a whole, mainly for the good of its people and its environment.

It is arguable as to whether his engineering work was solely for the good of man, as perhaps some of it was just to prove it could be done. A man of his means, such as Armstrong, could make anything happen in the Victorian era.

It is clear, that the machinery and building work attempted at Cragend Farm, was demonstrating what might be achieved if water were to be harnessed as a power for good; as a labour tool and as a power resource instead of coal.

Although it cannot be proved that his wish was to have electricity generated at the farm, it is clear that the No 490 was not only very capable of doing all its daily chores with the machinery, but also had enough power to operate a dynamo, if required, which in turn, would have charged a battery.

With his known love for the idea of electricity it is hard to argue that any of his projects were built without a thought for some sort of spark of electricity being a possibility.

The Hydraulic Silo is an unique building, with an amazing vision of what might be achieved through the use of water power, but the No 490 is the 'Big Daddy' at Cragend Farm, without which, none of what Armstrong was trying to achieve would have happened.

It is also worth noting that No 490 is a larger turbine than any remaining at Cragside at 30 H.P., and it arguably the oldest remaining Armstrong-Gilkes turbine in situ, having been installed in 1883. It was capable of generating 20 kw of electricity once again the highest wattage of all Armstrong's turbines.

Queen Victoria's reign was in its Golden era, and her empire was at it's peak.

The Industrial Revolution was also at the height of all its engineering glory, and those making money from it were becoming amongst the richest in the world.

Armstrong was arguabley the richest man in Europe.

Britain was a force to be reckoned with, having brilliant inventors, engineers, scientists, mathematicians and scholars all making an worldwide impact.

Cragend Farm stands as a symbol of how to use local resources and it is fair to say that we have a lot to learn from it as a demonstration centre both now and then.

Located in a rural area in the heart of Northumberland it is an honour and a pleasure to call it home.

Our time here as custodians of this unique site has been very rewarding and surprising, mainly to ourselves, who never expected to find such history right under our noses.

Many dignitaries came to visit the wider Cragside Estate to see the beautiful house, grounds and see 'The Magician' demonstrate his amazing hydraulic machines.

HRH The Prince and Princess of Wales (later King Edward VII and Queen Alexandra) stayed at Cragside in 1884. Well documented, it was a very high profile visit.

Less well documented was the fact that they also came to see Cragend Farm and the No 490 hydraulics there too. The Hydraulic Silo would have been in the process of being built at this point.

Newspaper articles cover it as a visit 'to his farm.

Diss Express and Norfolk & Suffolk Journal, September 8th 1884
An entry taken from 'The World' paper/magazine

'Rothbury is a pleasant old-fashioned village which nestles in the picturesque Coquetdale, at the foot of a range of heather clad hills. It is renowned in Northumberland as a health resort. Sir William Armstrong now possesses an estate of 15,000 acres in the neighbourhood. He began in 1860 by buying 7 acres of rocky hillside and mountain glen on which he built a cottage which has been expanded into the present house of Cragside. He bought Debdon Moor and the lakes which adorn it from the Duke of Northumberland then for £37,500, the Cartington estate from the Beck family, then Upper Trewitt purchased from the Smarts for £42,000 then Lower Trewitt for £50,000 and finally the Dawson's sold him Warton and property on which is the highest peak of Simonside. He has built about 15 model cottages at Rothbury for his labourers and at Craigend [Cragend] there is a large home farm on which is a very fine herd of short horns. This farm is about to be worked as experimentally by hydraulic machinery from a special reservoir upon a principal invented by Sir William.'

In 1888 The Princess Louisa (Queen Victoria's daughter) and her husband the Duke of Argyll came, and in many newspapers it is more closely explained:

Saturday 10th of November 1888 Newcastle Courant
(Royal Visit to Cragend 5th November 1888):
Her Royal Highness the Princess Louisa and the Marquis of Lorne, other guests of the Duke of Northumberland at Alnwick Castle, representatives of the city of Newcastle and others on Tuesday in response to the invitation of Lord and Lady Armstrong visited the lovely seat of the world famed engineer at Cragside Rothbury. The party from Alnwick Castle drove to Cragside in open carriages while the civic authorities left Newcastle and arrived at Rothbury by the 8:20 a.m. train. Arrived at Cragside walk was agreed upon and was

doubtless found to be an agreeable change alter the long ride extended over nearly two hours from Alnwick. The mansion is lighted at night by electricity and one of the first places visited was the house containing the engines for working the dynamos. From there the company walked around the hill to the Cragend Farm and examined The Silo. Subsequently they returned towards the house over the hill, from where a magnificent view was obtained. On Friday evening the Princess Louisa and the Marquis of Lorne after having being the guests of Their Graces the Duke and Duchess of Northumberland since Saturday evening left Alnwick Castle for London.

Taken from The British Newspaper Archives.

Chapter 12 The British Engineerium statement.

This section of the book is the additional information about the research that took place in and around our findings, which will help make sense of all the information we have found to date.

The British Engineerium's evaluation

Jonathan Minns [29] had evaluated the site for National Trust Cragside in the 1980's:

"...there is one complete and virtually intact Armstrong creation which, directly as a result of a design error on his behalf, remained virtually unused following it is believed, its second season. "

This is possibly not the case as the No 630 was added after its first use in 1884-1885.

Adjustments were made to Silo in 1886 on technical diagram.

Dated September 1st 1887 items for the turbine were ordered.

No 630 had 2100 rpm (!) and would have been capable of generating electricity.

Evidence
We also have verbal evidence that Joseph Gall an agricultural labourer was working there in 1890's because of census records.

A wonderful story, that came about from one of our tours, when Eileen Telfer and her daughter came to see the Silo. Eileen recalled that it had been passed down the generations that her Great Grandfather Joseph, had worked at the Silo. He had lived at Craghead opposite Cragend, and would walk to work down the hill, across the river Coquet, in summer on foot, or in winter on a boat, to work at Sir Williams Silo.

He had instructed his 10 year old daughter Agnes one day to wave a white sheet from their home at Craghead if her mother went into labour. That day, seeing the child waving the sheet, Joseph ran the two miles into Rothbury to fetch help, and then along the railway line to Craghead where his youngest son, Joseph was born.

We checked the census and found out that 1901 he had a three year old son named Joseph, and a thirteen year old daughter Agnes. That means Joseph Junior was born in 1898. The census also shows him living at Craghead in 1891, when Agnes was three. This piece of information is a fantastic insight into the dates the Silo was working. Catherine Cookson could not have made up a better tale of Victorian agricultural life.

Minns goes on to say ' ...as such, whilst it is not in the hands of the Trust it represents probably 'one of the finest purpose-built agricultural buildings in the world' and an illustrated reference would have to be made to it in the proposed museum as a brilliant example of his engineering innovations as applied throughout his farming interests. "

Cragend Farm History Tours take a look at the history of the farm from the Big Bang right through to the 21st century.

It is a sensory experience with guests encouraged to touch the machines and feel the history.

The Armstrong Turbines List:
(courtesy of Gilkes, Kendal)

No 395 c1859 sold to W.G. Armstrong

No 428 29th April 1881 sold to W.G. Armstrong

No 431 June 1881 sold to W.G. Armstrong

No 444 18th December 1881 sold to Sir W.G. Armstrong (Netherton)

No 464 October 1882 sold to Sir W.G. Armstrong

No 490 31st August 1883 sold to Sir W.G. Armstrong (Cragend)

No 491 4th September 1883 sold to Sir W.G. Armstrong (Trewitt)

No 572 March 1886 sold to Sir W.G. Armstrong (Power House)

No 630 September 1st 1887 sold to Lord W.G. Armstrong (Cragend)

No 1306
 Hydraulic Hoist technical drawing dated August 1884.

See the Gilkes record books.

References followed by Further Reading:

I have tried were possible to tag the references in order to assist with further reading. This is not a definitive list but is here to suggest further reading. There is some repertiton in order to join sections.

[1] James Whitelaw
OCCUPATION: Engineer, Hydraulic engineer, Inventor
NATIONALITY: Scottish; British
BORN IN: Scotland, United Kingdom
Inventor of Reaction Turbine; based in Glasgow; worked in Paisley, Scotland with James Stirrat, patented an improved version of Barker's mill in 1841 in England and 1843 in America; it became known as the Scotch turbine, and is regarded as the first true metal turbine water wheel; Whitelaw patented La Cour's improvement of the bottom-feeding of the supply water, adding spiral curved arms decreasing in cross-section from wheel opening to jet; 1843 - American patent (#3,153) claims the proportioning of these arms as his patentable improvement; Scotch turbine was manufactured in Europe and America by a number of firms from the 1840s - early 1870s;

[2] Gilkes turbine small one for the laundry? How did he know this? Is this No ? Or is it the dairy one?

[3] Henrietta Heald/Peter McKenzie Authors of Lord Armstrong biographies.

[4] https://premium.weatherweb.net/weather-in-history-1850-to-1899-ad/

[5] The inventor of the Vortex Turbine was Professor James Thomson (1822-92) of Queen's College in Belfast, and he patented the design in 1850. The first Vortex turbine in England was supplied to James Cropper who owned paper mills in Burneside near Kendal. This was manufactured by a Belfast firm working under the supervision of Prof. Thomson. The Williamson Brothers acquired a license to manufacture the turbines from Prof. Thomson who supplied them with drawings and explained the design principles. Although this license was not

exclusive, Williamson Brothers manufactured many more turbines than any other company.

[6] In 1853 two brothers named Williamson established a company at Canal Head, Kendal. The first turbine they built in 1856 was installed at Holmescales Farm at Old Hutton and powered farm machinery there for more than a century. This, the "Williamson Bros Vortex Turbine No. 1 taken from the invention of Thomson. In 1881 Gilbert Gilkes (1845-1924) bought Williamson Brothers. In 1932 the company acquired James Gordon & Co, and became Gilbert Gilkes & Gordon.

[7] https://etc.usf.edu/clipart/27100/27133/reaction_tur_27133.htm
Tangent turbine. Encyclopaedia Britannica, 1893
"Professor James Thomson's inward flow or vortex turbine has been selected as the type of reaction turbines. It is one of the best even in normal conditions of working, and the mode of regulation introduced is decidedly superior to that in most reaction turbines; it might almost be said to be the only mode of regulation which satisfies the conditions of efficient working, and it has been adopted in a modified form in the Leffel turbine, which is now largely used in America. The turbine has suction pipes, which permit the turbine to be placed at any height less than 30 feet above the tail-water level. The water enters the turbine by cast-iron supply pipes at A, and is discharged through two suction pipes S. The water on entering the case distributes itself through a rectangular supply chamber SC, from which it finds its way equally to the four guide-blade passages G. In these passages it acquires a velocity about equal to that due to half the fall, and is directed into the wheel at an angle of about 10 or 12 degrees with the tangent to its circumference. The wheel W receives the water in equal proportions from each guide-blade passage." — Encyclopaedia Britannica, 1893

[8] Tom Hay: c1980's North East Mills Magazine
https://northeastmills.wordpress.com/mill-research/cragend-a-peculiar-turbine/
Tom Hay a former Vickers Armstrong employee who visited Cragend Farm some while ago thought that it was a vortex turbine without guide vanes but now realise it is something completely unlike any turbine seen anywhere.

It is an impulse type with an angled top entry, and with the water discharge out of the rectangular base. There is a pulley belt drive on the far side which would have had thick belt coiled on it, behind the inlet pipe.

In the February letter there is a reference to the 30hp turbine Gilkes No 490, which is still insitu today, and drove a threshing machine and other equipment.

The March letter refers to a turbine to drive a "chaff cutter" to chop green forage to make silage and Gilkes strongly recommends their "tangent turbine" with an adjusting nozzle rather than their "re-action" wheel.

Letter from Giles to Armstrong dated 4th July 1884 [11]

Dear Sir
The tangent turbine for Crag End is almost finished. In yours of the 7th of March you stated that until the chaff cutter is fixed in position you cannot determine the length of shaft. On the 4th May you say it should be of sufficient length to take two pulleys. We think that by this time you will have fixed the position of the chaff cutter and to avoid any mistake in respect to the length of the shaft we beg to say that unless we hear from you it will be made as per sketch.
We remain yours faithfully, Gilbert Gilkes.

[9] Hydraulic Silo Building, Cragend Farm, Rothbury Solstice Heritage Report 2020

[10] ARS Archaeological report Cragend Farm 2012 Dr G Scott

[11] Tyne & Wear Archives Discovery Museum Newcastle upon Tyne

[12] Henry Watson - maker of the Newcastle upon Tyne Swing Bridge.
1767 Watson's High Bridge Works was established
1846 Henry Watson inherits the family business at High Bridge Works.
Visionary Newcastle inventor Lord Armstrong commissioned Watson

to produce the rotary engine that pioneered the use of hydroelectricity.

[13] The British Engineerium: Museum in Brighton conservators of engineering used by NT Cragside. https://en.wikipedia.org/wiki/British_Engineerium

[14] Historic England listings: https://historicengland.org.uk/listing/the-list/list-entry/1153196

[15] Trewitt Turbine No 491 now located at Cragside - exploded and restored to see the internal workings.

[16] Cragside National Trust Property, Rothbury, Northumberland. The remaining turbines and waterwheel are located at the Power House.

[17] Professor John Wrightson was a leading writer, British agriculturalist and book writer in the 1800's. He created Downton Agricultural College and is thought to have been one of the first to try to make silage. https://en.wikipedia.org/wiki/John_Wrightson

[18] Cragend Farm was also named as 'Home Farm' by newspaper articles and other researchers such as J. Minns. This appears to be their error based on references about the Home Farm that is named on the OS maps of 1898 nearer the Cragside house. It may be that Lord Armstrong referred to Cragend Farm as 'Home Farm' in the 1870's onwards, which led to later confusion when trying to dissect information about the Silo.

[19] Historic Houses Funded emergency work to the Silo and mentored The Renwick's in showcasing the history of the farm.

[20] Tyne & Wear Archives Discovery Museum Newcastle upon Tyne

[21] Encyclopaedia Brittanica:

[22] Invented by William Armstrong and exhibited at The Great Exhibition 1851 [27] and went on to be used in Tower bridge in London

[23] Sheffield tool maker W A Tyzack Stellar Works Cragend Farm 2023.

[24] Letter from Gilkes to Armstrong . 1st Feb 1884

Dear Sir

30 HP Turbine [Cragend No 490 Ordered 1883 see order form]

We note your instructions and shall take care to have a strong shaft.

Threshing machine

We enclose a sketch the size of the opening in the floor which the large machine will require. The A8. 6 horse machine (Netherton/Trewitt?) 42-inch drum has thrashed the quantity named? and has exceeded it taking a day's work through so we have no doubt about it.

The screen already sent? will do very well for the large machine.

The dressing machine and the elevators are too small in our judgement for the wider machine there will be sufficient power to drive the wider machine with barley awner increased length, of elevators and dressing machine in proportion.

We can deliver in about 21 days and as time is of importance, we have just the machine in hand but wait your instructions. As to the dressing machine, screen, two elevators and barley awner. If you remove the whole 4 HP plant to Cragend the cost of the new 6 HP plant would be as follows:

A 8 machine	£56 -0-0
Barley Awner	£7- 0-0
2 elevators	£14 - 0 − 0
A1 Corbett dresser (threshing)	£12 - 7 shillings 6 pence
Screen 4. 3 and 16-inches	£14 -10 shillings 0 pence

spindle coupling & wall box and pedestal   £4 - 3 shillings and 6 pence

£108 and 1 shilling

If you do not require the screen at Cragend the total will be £93 and 11 shillings [£93.11.0]

Trusting that we may be favoured with your early reply
We are
Yours respectfully
Gilbert Gilkes
Late Williamson Bros.

[25] Hydraulic Accumulator: A hydraulic accumulator is a pressure storage reservoir in which an incompressible hydraulic fluid is held under pressure that is applied by an external source of mechanical energy. The external source can be an engine, a spring, a raised weight, or a compressed gas. See also Tower Bridge and Camden Tower.
http://www.glias.org.uk/journals/8-c.html

[26] https://en.wikipedia.org/wiki/Henry_Pooley_%26_Son
https://collection.sciencemuseumgroup.org.uk/people/cp3531/henry-pooley-and-son-limited

[27] https://en.wikipedia.org/wiki/Great_Exhibition

[28] 1871 Ploughing Competition at Cragend with 40 teams of horse drawn ploughs. Organised by Sir William. Ask Roger.

Re Iron Age Fort
 Pike heads and spur found at Crag End Hill; HER ID 2947; NGR NU 0766 0190. LiDAR Pritchard.
https://archaeologydataservice.ac.uk/archsearch/record.xhtml

[29] Jonathan Minns British Engineerium. His report 1985 for Cragside NT: A good guess at the general idea of it all but not necessarily correct.

'Home Farm: At Home Farm [he means Cragend Farm here] there is one complete and virtually intact Armstrong creation which, directly as a result of a design error on his behalf, remained virtually unused following it is believed, its second season. As such, whilst it is not in the hands of the Trust it represents probably 'one of the finest purpose-built agricultural buildings in the world' and an illustrated reference would have to be made to it in the proposed museum as a brilliant example of his engineering innovations as applied throughout his farming interests.

It is a stone-walled silo consisting of two large cement rendered tanks with corrugated wrought iron arched roofs in exceptionally good condition. Directly under the roof trusses is a serious of beams with interspaced pulleys. These in turn carried chains designed to lift the circular one ton granite weights used for compressing the silage. The chains were powered by a typical Armstrong hydraulic intensifier housed in the lower section of the central Tower separating the two silos. Above the high ground floor access is a small Thompson vortex turbine which was used for either a grain sifter or crusher. Essentially the machinery is all there and intact and indeed the intensifier has probably not been visited for nearly 100 years owing to access. The whole complex could in fact be either mothballed or the two prime movers be excavated and restored for museum. The entire exercise however merits detailed consideration within the whole project and provided adequate skilled supervision were involved could be done relatively cheaply as a youth training exercise.

James Whitelaw: James Whitelaw | Science Museum Group Collection

Difference between reaction and impulse turbines: How turbines work | Impulse and reaction turbines (explainthatstuff.com)

A video explaining Francis and Pelton turbine designs: Comparison of Pelton, Francis & Kaplan Turbine (youtube.com)

[30] Professor George Irlam : Armstrong's Pump House research

[31] Cragside engineer John Allen ' I'd say that all the ones I've seen are vortex types. Certainly, all of ours at Cragside are, they all have the control mechanisms.'
[32] Diss Express 1884 Craigend Farm [Cragend] visited by Prince and Princess of Wales while staying at Cragside:

'Rothbury is a pleasant old-fashioned village which nestles in the pictures Coquetdale, at the foot of a range of heather clad hills. It is renowned in Northumberland as a health resort. Sir William Armstrong now possesses an estate of 15,000 acres in the neighbourhood. He began in 1860 by buying 7 acres of rocky hillside and mountain glen on which he built a cottage which has been expanded into the present house of Cragside. He bought Debdon Moor and the lakes which adorn it from the Duke of Northumberland then for £37,500, the Cartington estate from the Beck family, then Upper Trewitt purchased from the Smarts for £42,000 then Lower Trewitt for £50,000 and finally the Dawson's sold him Warton and property on which is the highest peak of Simonside. He has built about 15 model cottages at Rothbury for his labourers and at Craigend [Cragend] there is a large home farm on which is a very fine herd of short horns. This farm is about to be worked as experimentally by hydraulic machinery from a special reservoir upon a principal invented by Sir William.'

Chapter 13

The Cragend Farm version of Lord Armstrongs Life

- 1810 Born Newcastle-upon[Tyne
- Armstrong was mentored by Mr. Armourer Donkin (London Lawyer, also a Newcastle and Rothbury landowner) from the age of 7, and at 17 was taken to Lincolns Inn London to train to be a lawyer.
- Armstrong was friends with Henry Watson (who worked at family firm Newcastle High Bridge Works 1848 – designing the Swing Bridge 1876)
- Armstrong practiced law for decades, but engineering was his true passion, and in 1851 when Donkin died and left him money and land in Rothbury, he worked full time on hydro-powered machinery.
- In 1851 Armstrong exhibited his Hydraulic Hoist at The Great Exhibition in London, along side others such as H. Pooley & Sons who was exhibiting his weighbridge.
- His work in building reservoirs in Newcastle to assist with clean water, to stop the cholera epidemic, is well documented.
- Already a wealthy lawyer, the Hydraulic machinery was an success, and after patenting it, he went on to produce many more at The Elswick Works Newcastle, and became very successful financially.
- The Crimean War (October 1853 to February 1856) intervened when HM Government request his help to make armaments (much like Dyson with ventilators during Covid) and Armstrong became the main arms dealer for Britain's Government during this time.
- Once the war was over the Government released his contract. He was put out by this snub, and sought contracts from elsewhere in the world, and became a world arms dealer to Russia, China, Brazil, America, India, Japan etc. (This is ethically a wince part for many).
- He was by now a multi-millionaire even by todays standards. They said he was, 'the richest man in Europe!'

- In 1863, apparently exhausted by all the business of his 'Business' he returns to Rothbury, and purchases a shooting lodge on Cragend Hill to build a modern mansion.
- He used the Debdon Burn to power engineering inventions on hydraulics such as his Pump House and his electric system by 1878 at Tumbleton Lake.
- The Debdon Burn dried up c1866 and he needed another source of water so he firstly leased land from Duke of Northumberland finally taking over Cragend Farm which borders The Blackburn to the east of the estate.
- He then had access to free flowing water that was high on the top of the crags. He made reservoirs and the water flowed in pipes from these lakes to his machinery.
- As many of the great and the good in Victorian times, he bought a herd of prize Beef Shorthorn cattle and housed them at Cragend.
- He ordered numerous turbines from Gilbert Gilkes and they were working at Cragside and also at Cragend, Trewitt and Netherton Farms in 1880s.
- The Silo was constructed to make silage for his cattle in 1884.
- There are numerous Newspaper articles about a Royal Visits to Cragend in 1884 and1888 and several Newspaper articles about the Silo and how it worked in 1890
- Armstrong died in 1900 December 27th.

Chapter 14

Armstrongs Contemporaries worth noting, some of whom he met and was aquainted with:

- Robert Stephenson 1803-1859 Father of the Railways
- George Cruddas 1791-1879 Local Ship owner and Investor in Armstrong's engineering
- Prof. John Wrightson agriculturalist and journalist 1840-1916
- The Great Exhibition Crystal Palace 1st May 1851 – 15th October 1851
- Nikola Tesla 1856-1943 Physicist and inventor Dynamos and Wireless transmissions
- Thomas Edison 1847-1931 Inventor (DC electricity, light bulb etc)
- George Westinghouse 1846-1914 inventor engineer (AC electricity)
- Joseph Swan 1828-1914 – Chemist inventor of Incandescent light bulb
- Isambard Kingdom Brunel (1806-1859) Engineer GWR Bridgesetc
- Michael Faraday (1791-1867) Scientist in electrochemistry and electrocmagnetism
- Humphrey Davy (1778-1829) Chemist inventor of Davy Lamp and electrochemistry
- Joseph Bramah (1748-1814) Inventor of the Hydraulic Press
- Prof. James Thomson (1822-1892) Inventor of the Turbine Brother of Lord Kelvin!
- Williamson Brothers & Gilbert Gilkes (1865-1895): Producers of the Thomson turbine.
- Li Hongzhang Cragside visit 1896 (Chief Chinese Diplomat of Qing dynasty)
- H.M. King Edward VII

Chapter 15

A Do-er-up-er - The Renwicks uncover the history.

My husband Shaun & I moved from Holystone Estates Farm, in Upper Coquetdale in 2010 with our sons, dogs and a large amount of old Victorian furniture that wouldn't sell at auction:

We bought Cragend Farm in a dilapidated state in 2011 without planning permission after much deliberation, seeing it as a farm with the possibility to continue farming.

The prospectus said "has potential" but exactly what for was unclear.

The only building of historical note on the details was the Grade II* Hydraulic Silo linked to Cragside but ......The Weighbridge, the Machine Room and The Turbine Room were just classed as outbuildings with no hint of any history.

There was no reference to the Iron Age/Romano/Anglo Saxon settlement.

There were no visible signs of historic artefacts anywhere on site. However, now we can piece much more history together.

A potted history of Cragend Farm – the Cragend Version

- Ice Age Glacial Deposits   400 million years ago Silurian Period
- Later Prehistoric Settlement (4000BC to 43AD) Stone/Bronze/Iron Age 3300 BC – 1200 BC
- Celtic Camp/Votadini (British Pre-historic Tribe) – Romans (43 to 410) – Anglo Saxons
- King Edward III and The Percy Family 1331
- Wars of the Roses 1455-1487
- Border Wars (c1299-c1601).
- Enclosures began in the 12th century (1100-1200) and proceeded rapidly in the period 1450–1640
- The Jacobite's / Georgians (1714–1837) Rothbur Registers
- Duke of Northumberland: Patent, leases and surveying pre-OS 1331-1873
- Lord Armstrong of Cragside (tenant then owner c1873 - 2011)
- The Thompsons tenant farmers to the Armstrong's of Bamburgh c1902-2009
- The Renwick Family 2011-Present Owners.

Chapter 16

Celtic Camp reference : A quote from 1855 document:

"Passing about one mile east from 'Reivers Well' we come to
'Cragend' one of Sir Williams farm, where some fine stock may be
seen"…."Directly north, across the field from the cattle boxes there is
the remains of a Celtic Camp, 37 yards diameter with some rampart,
some parts of it 3 feet high and one fosse of some depth. There are
several circle houses inside, 7 to 9 feet diameter. Altogether this has
been a dwelling of some importance both as to strength and
situation."
A Guide to Rothbury and Surrounding District by an unknown author
in 1885 (attrib: Rev A. Scott)

Official LiDar Site Details backs this up :

- Cragend Farm Romano-British homestead (Cartington)
- In the early 20th century a small enclosure was noted north of
  Cragend Farm and a quern was discovered nearby. It is not
  clear whether the whole enclosure was visible at this time, but
  by the 1970s only the southern part remained. The enclosure
  may have been a Romano-British homestead and it originally
  measured about 28m in diameter. The edges are marked by a
  bank of earth and stone, with traces of a ditch in places.
- Reference number:
- N2910
- Historical periods:
- Roman (43 to 410)
- Later Prehistoric (4000BC to 43AD).
- Event(s):
- FIELD OBSERVATION, Ordnance Survey Archaeology Division
  Field Investigation 1976; B H Pritchard

A Roman ,cast lead steel yard weight, dating to AD 43-410 was found
in 2024 amongst other items by metal detectorists at Cragend Farm.

The weight is bi-conical and would have had a (now missing) iron loop protruding from the top. The sight of the missing loop is evidenced by an area of embedded iron and corrosion product. There are multiple striations and scuff marks on the surface. The weight is a light cream colour with an area of orange-brown iron corrosion at the top. Ours is the same as one at The British Museum.

Our Title Deeds were non-existant:
We tried to find our title deeds but Cragside NT, and Bamburgh both said they did not have any. Alnwickj Castle however, came up with an amazing document which basically is their title deeds from King Edwards III. They said that we would have been included on this this deed.

The patent is basically a note to the Kings friend John de Clavering in 1331. Written in Latin, Northumberland Archives thankfully gave me a translation, and this is loosely what it says:

Dear John,
You have no issue so I am going to give all my lands that you look after for me in Rothbury and Warkworth, to my next best friend Henry, on your death. OK!
Love Edward.

An ancient map of The Rothbury Estate from The Northumberland Estates Archives shows Cragend clearly.
The Order of the Garter and Coat of Arms suggest it is 1380-1460 and although Alnwick Castle can not be sure of the date, they have no reason to believe otherwise; possibly it had been re drawn later from an early map from that date.

Enclosures began in the 12th century (1100-1200) and proceeded rapidly in the period 1450–1640. The rubbing stones on the farm are placed in the fields to stop the cattle rubbing he fences. We have over eight in many fields.

Maps:

We have been fortunate to have access to a number of older maps than just Ordanance Survey. The National Library for Scotland hold the only two OS maps for the Armstrong era of 1864 and 1898 and there was not an OS map by then before this time. However, the Duke of Northumberlands Estates were very efficient at keeping records of their lands over many centuries, and we have had access to some of them.

1380-1460 : ancient map of Rothbury and the region showing Cragend. Likely to have been updated by Norton.

An Armstrong map circa 1770 shows Craig End (Cragend)
Not much is known about the Mapmakers Andrew and Mostyn Armstrong but the link is not lost on us... is it? see John Strawhorn article on the mapmakers.

We were allowed access to a 1781 Leighton (Lighton) and Watson Lease from Northumberland Estates. The Watsons were at Bamburgh but its not clear if these are the same Watsons.

There is a 1800 map of part of Cragend Farm showing a Foot Road through Cragend Hill and a sheep fold.

Fry's Map of 1820 has Cragend shown on it.

There is also a 1831 Map of part of Cragend End Farm and Dover Farm by Surveyor Thomas Bell showing Rothbury North Forest ie Cragend Hill.

Chapter 17

The Cragend Buildings:

The Cooling Room and Jostle Stones:

A 19th century invention to stop cart wheels hitting buildings in busy areas, Jostle Stones or Glancing Stones or Guard Stones were, and can still be seen today on some buildings in Britain.

This is an extract from Cragend Farm ARS report building O:
The Milking shed/ Cooling Room

- *4.16.3 External east facing elevation (Fig 204)*
- *This single-storey, elevation is constructed of sandstone ashlar broken rangework and is completed at its northern extent by a matching set of long and short punch-faced quoins with drafted margins (see Fig. 204)...The original door opening is constructed of matching, chamfered, long and short punch-faced quoins with drafted margins and a chamfered lintel. **<u>A "glancing" stone is placed at the foot of the northern corner of this elevation, indicating an expectation of significant amounts of cart traffic in this area</u>**. This may be a function of its position in proximity to the Threshing Stead.*
- *4.16.6 Phase 1: c. 1870*
- *The first phase of construction of Building O is the construction of the loosebox with a single door, wide enough for stock, at its south east corner. The building was an extension to the earlier Building H. It is considered likely that the loosebox is roughly contemporary in date to the development of Buildings K, L and M, based on the similarity in construction and finish. The tentative date for this is somewhat speculative, but is based on the incomplete plan shown on the first edition OS map, produced in around 1866. The interpretation of the building as a loosebox is based on its structural form and association with the other buildings of the farm complex. It is possible that, along with Buildings K, L and M, it might be seen*

as part of a reaction to a requirement to increase the amount of cattle at the farm at that time.

The guard stones are a feature of busy farm life, but it is unclear as to whether it was an Armstrong addition or had been placed there ore his intervention.

Based on influences of Richard Norman Shaw it is likely these were added as a smart solution to protecting the Ashlar stone buildings from day to day wear and tear on them.

Glancing stones at Crgend Farm.

The Courtyard and Dairies

The Dairies were added on by The Duke of Northumberland in the 1800's (OS 1848)

The hemels (hemmel) , or hovels are the arches along the whole east/west line of the building and would have been where the agricultural labourer's lived up until possibly WWII.

The middle dairy was removed to expose the original arches 2013.

The farm graffiti is located on the top floor of the granary above the arches, and comprises of over 500 inscriptions dating from 1860s.

There is also graffiti in the Silo dating back to the 1890s

The dairies with the heavy horses in the foreground. Circa 1935
Note the finials on the top of the slate roof. Latterly the roof was
asbestos and the finials were all nowhere to be found.

These finials are the same as the ones on the cattle sheds at the rear
of the farm and also on other parts of the Cragside Estate. We assume
they were made as ventilation for the sheds, and are of cast iron,
probably made at Elswick Works, Newcastle.

They have Welsh slate on the roof, with a wooden shingle beneath
them. It is arguable that once again Richard Norman Shaws influence
followed on to these designs on the roof, which are decorative as well
as practical, being for ventilation. The huts or sheds are wooden
structures made of whole tree trunks.

Named, 'The Ginnel,' meaning a walled alley, (page 58) the pillowed
edged stoned walkway is the same as at Cragside main drive in the
and under the main arch. It is edged by buildings and walls, and was
a place to parade the cattle. There are stories of men in show jackets
leading the cows on bridles along the Ginnel, to show them off to
Armstrong and his friends.

Chapter 18. Planning Permission

Planning required an archaeological report, and ours is the size of a family bible.
Archaeologists, found that much of the farm is much older than Armstrong, dating it from OS maps and mapmakers Armstrong, Fry and Bennett etc. The Conservation officer had given strict guidance about the Grade II* listed building and on further inspection also the other discovered turbine.

The oldest section was a house barn or 'safe house' with no windows, but high walls and ceiling and one large door. A mezzanine style floor inside would have been for people to sleep above their animals, much as in a pele or bastle tower. Other similar are dotted along the Coquet including ruins at Hope.

Housebarns were built from prehistoric times after people discovered that the body heat of animals helps to warm human living areas.
It also prevented thieves from stealing their animals.
Housebarns were developed in western Europe, Scandinavia, and the British Isles and continued being built into the 19th century.
There is a ruined Bastle at Hope, and it is arguable that Cragend was originally some sort of Bastle, as these houses are a type of construction found along the Anglo-Scottish border, in the areas formerly plagued by border reivers. They are fortified farmhouses, characterized by security measures against raids.
The characteristics of Cragend's housebarn are similar to that of the classic bastle house are extremely thick stone walls (about 1 metre thick), ☑ with the ground floor devoted to stable space for the most valuable animals, ☑ and a vaulted stone or flat timber floor between it ☑ and the first floor with internal access such as a stairway or ladder. ☑ .

The House Barn work on the interior exposed a witches mark near the door edge. These were engraved into the stone lintels or marked in charcoal to ward off eveil spitits that may want to come in through the door.

The Cattle sheds and Tackroom

There were out-buildings pre-Armstrong, mainly a Calving Shed, as listed on tenancy leases.

Armstrong changed nearly all the buildings for his requirements. He added an extra dairy. He added a cooling room for the dairy. He added a machine room, a turbine room and a threshing barn and granary. He also added 70 stalls for cattle, all made from wood with slate roof and metal finials.

There were Clydesdale heavy horses working the land and there was also stabling and a tack room.

The Bull Pen was where the bull lived. A stone building with a slate roof and high stone walls. One door, an interior gate and an exterior gate.

The Machine Room

The Machine Room was originally a Gin-Gan (a horse powered circular room).

It was demolished and replaced by The Machine Room in the 1880's by Armstrong to house the machinery that was linked to the turbine No 490.

There is a hole in the wall that was for the giant drive belts that fitted to the machines.

There is some discrepancy on the name 'Home Farm'.

On the OS maps it is marked as the now Visitor Centre at Cragside, but many of the newspaper articles refer to Cragend Farm a Home Farm too.

We think it is a newspaper editorial mistake, that in local terms became muddled into the history of Cragside

Cragend Farmhouse

Cragend Farmhouse is a 17th century two up two down, similar to many in Northumberland.

The Duke of Northumberland made amendments to it throughout the centuries, and these are listed in leases dating back to 1730's.

Cragend Farm Lease 1848 for Carmichael lists amogst other items:

Dwelling house consisting four rooms in front & back kitchen
- Dairy and servants room behind with a privy
- Ash pit and coal house attached
- Five stall stables and Hayhouse
- A byre for eight cows a calf house
- Poultry house 2 piggeries with Folds
- Barn and fodder house - Granary
- Hovel of two arches with fold in front
- Hovel of one arch with fold in front

Latterly, the piggeries, coal and ash hole were altered by Armstrong and turned into a wash house with coal fuels wash pot.

In 1953 many of the Cragside properties were updated for the arrival of the Emperor of Japan's son, who stayed at Cragside during the time of HRH Queen Elizabeth II coronation. Staff stayed at Cragend so that his entourage could stay in their quarters in Cragside.

Cragend Farmhouse had the wash house with coal fired wash pot, which was split in half, to create a downstairs bathroom with bath toilet and hand basin but no heating!

Cragend Farmhouse, Cragend Farm 1912
with William Thompson courtesy Mr. G Thompson

Cragend Wash Pot

Chapter 19

Waiting....

Whilst waiting for Planning Permission we got on with other areas and this is a short version of our progress:

Cragend Farm was purchased on April Fools Day 2011
While waiting we got on with clearing the site.

The Turbine Room and The Machine Room: Hidden in a small area at the back of the barns was a machine, covered in muck and debris, which turned out to be a turbine. No 490 30 H.P. 1300rpm. 200kw. 190 ft head of water from Blackburn Lake.

An Australian visitor with the family name Carmichael knocked on the door, and showed us her heritage on a census form linked to this area and this farm. This led to some research as to how old Cragend Farm really is.

This included a search of The Rothbury Registers where, from 1643, Births Deaths and Marriages record Cragend history.
This then led to the first of several searches at The Northumberland Estates Archives and some detective work.

We put in a large planning application that covered all the buildings on the farm 27th July 2011.
- We knew that as the Silo is listed it that it would not be a smooth journey!
- It is a Building at Risk classed as Very Poor.
- We were given over 18 conditions to fulfil, with the focus on The Silo being first on the list… to repair the slate roof!
- Work started in early February 2012.
- A large chunk of our budget went out the window.
- The moment the work was done on 2nd March 2012 permission was granted.

Opening to the Public

In 2015 and 4 years of building work we decided to have an open Day to show Rothbury, and anyone free that day, what we were aiming to achieve.

Anthea Logan Wood came along to the cookery demonstration and brought with her these fabulous photographs, and also much history from her memories her as a child.

George Thompson has also been kind enough to give us many photographs of his family here over the years.

However, we had a Listed Building with a roof but without any floors and the machinery was hanging precariously from the joists.

So, we decided to take further action.

Chapter 20

The Royal Visits to Cragend Farm

Many dignitaries came to visit The Cragside Estate to see the beautiful house, grounds and see 'The Magician' demonstrate his amazing hydraulic machines.

HRH Prince and Princess of Wales (later King Edward VII and Queen Alexandra) stayed at Cragside in 1884. Well documented, it was a very high profile visit.

Less well documented was the fact that they also came to see Cragend Farm and the No 490 hydraulics there too. The Hydraulic Silo would have been in the process of being built at this point. Newspaper articles cover it as a visit 'to his farm'.

Diss Express and Norfolk & Suffolk Journal, September 8th 1884 & From 'The World' paper/magazine
The Prince and Princess of Wales …. Rothbury is a pleasant old-fashioned village which nestles in the pictures Coquetdale, at the foot of a range of heather clad hills. It is renowned in Northumberland as a health resort. Sir William Armstrong now possesses an estate of 15,000 acres in the neighbourhood. He began in 1860 by buying 7 acres of rocky hillside and mountain glen on which he built a cottage which has been expanded into the present house of Cragside. He bought Debdon Moor and the lakes which adorn it from the Duke of Northumberland then for £37,500, the Cartington estate from the Beck family, then Upper Trewitt purchased from the Smarts for £42,000 then Lower Trewitt for £50,000 and finally the Dawson's sold him Warton and property on which is the highest peak of Simonside. He has built about 15 model cottages at Rothbury for his labourers and at Craigend [Cragend] there is a large home farm on which is a very fine herd of short horns. This farm is about to be worked as experimentally by hydraulic machinery from a special reservoir upon a principal invented by Sir William.

In 1888 The Princess Louisa (Queen Victoria's daughter) and her husband the Duke of Argyll came, and in many newspapers it is more closely explained.

Saturday 10th of November 1888 Newcastle Courant
(Royal Visit to Cragend 5th November 1888):

Her Royal Highness the Princess Louisa and the Marquis of Lorne, other guests of the Duke of Northumberland at Alnwick Castle, representatives of the city of Newcastle and others on Tuesday in response to the invitation of Lord and Lady Armstrong visited the lovely seat of the world famed engineer at Cragside Rothbury. The party from Alnwick Castle drove to Cragside in open carriages while the civic authorities left Newcastle and arrived at Rothbury by the 8:20 a.m. train. Arrived at Cragside walk was agreed upon and was doubtless found to be an agreeable change alter the long ride extended over nearly two hours from Alnwick. The mansion is lighted at night by electricity and one of the first places visited was the house containing the engines for working the dynamo's. From there the company walked around the hill to the Cragend Farm and examined The Silo. Subsequently they returned towards the house over the hill, from where a magnificent view was obtained. On Friday evening the Princess Louisa and the Marquis of Lorne after having being the guests of Their Graces the Duke and Duchess of Northumberland since Saturday evening left and it castle for London.

Chapter 21

More repair work

In 2019 we started to apply for a grant to help us repair more of the Silo. Until this point everything had been privately funded.

It is arguable that we made an error in not applying for grants when we had saved cash but it was a naïve error. Most grants require you to pay up to 50% yourself. However, you can be slightly held to ransom if you receive a grant, with conditions attached.

We were turned down for a National Lottery Grant because we have private ownership not a charity. Luckily, a very KIND Historic England employee suggested we talk to Historic Houses (called Country Houses Association back then).

We applied and a committee of people came out to see the Silo. That day they also went to visit Seaton Delaval NT property. They realised immediately that an emergency grant was needed to save the machinery from falling some 30 feet into the Silo tower and approved it immediately.

Grant funding Visit to Cragend Farm
Country Houses and Historic Houses Committee visit July 2018
(N.Hudson et al)

There has been lots of teamwork at Cragend Farm, but when we had to repair the floors, it ramped up a level.

We used local joiners and stonemasons to help us, and a very brave Storey and Edmonsdson builder (a.k.a. Graham Bates) to help us put an RSJ with 'ratchet straps' in the top floor to hold the No 630 turbine while we mended the floors.

The new floors and staircase made it possible to have visitors inside the Silo finally.

Thanks to HH we were able to run tours of the farm for people to see the machinery and learn its history

Peter McKenzie, an employee of Vickers Armstrong and their curator, came to visit, exclaiming that he had no idea that the Silo existed and he thought he knew all about Armstrong. He had even written a book about Armstrong!

He suggested the drawing for this building might be in The Tyne and Wear Museum, as he had personally put all the drawings there himself. But we needed some information.

We received a small grant from The Catherine Cookson Trust and used it for the archaeologists to come back in 2020 to assess the engine tower of the Silo building.

They surveyed The Tower and produced a document that enforces the original documents from 2012.

And they found a number on the machinery …. No 1306!!!

So finally I could go to The Discovery Museum, Tyne & Wear Archives, and try and find the drawing.

It took many months of negotiation and research but finally after years of searching for something of substance relating to Armstrong and Cragend I found it!

Rolls of technical drawings from the Armstrong Vickers Archive.
Tyne & Wear Museum archive room February 2023.
Credit Tyne & Wear Museum.

Other than Cragside's main house and garden in 1953 , most of Cragside was listed later in 1987.

Historic England also listed the Cragend Farm Hydraulic Silo building in 1987 despite it not being National Trust property but still under the ownership of the Armstrongs of Bamburgh.

Jonathan Minns, then working for National Trust as a consultant said Crgaend Farm Hydraulic Silo represents probably 'one of the finest purpose-built agricultural buildings in the world' ... 'a brilliant example of his [Armstrongs] engineering innovations as applied throughout his farming interests'.

Built in 1884 it was connected to the Turbine Room by means of pipework and housed a 1 ton hoist for lifting 36 large stone weights.

There are 18 weights in each bay of the Silo. They were used to squash the grass and pickle it into silage.

In 1886 he decided to add a second bay with extra weights and a turbine,
No 630 is a 3 hp Thomson turbine for cutting grass using a chaff cutter.

The technical drawing gives us new information on the machine.
It is described as 'The Giant' and it is over 17 feet tall when fully extended (9 ft plus 8ft 3 inches).
It has a south inlet pipe and is attached by a conical pipe network to no 630 turbine on the first floor.
It worked at lifting 18 weights all weighing 1 ton each un into the roof of the buildings bays.

The technical drawing is waxed linen and comes from the Armstrong-Vickers archives; it would have been the technical drawing for the engineering side of construction of the building.

The diagram is labelled:
> Sir W. G. Armstrong Cragside 1 Ton Hoist.

This gives some idea of date as he was not made a Lord until 1887. The archaeologists had suspected that the building was built in sections, and the diagram shows that the tower and east bay were built first. The second bay is likely to have been added later once they knew that the building operated sufficiently. The building is more balanced with both silo bays, and may have been an homage to the Border Reivers as he was an Armstrong.

The dates on the drawing are vitally important.

The notation 'Erecting plan sent 26/8/84' gives us some idea that the building work was happening in 1884 which is over a decade earlier than first thought by Historic England who had dated it c1895. This has now been amended due to this document.

There are three drawings on the diagram; one showing an overhead view, a view from the east and a view from the west. These drawings are coloured and covered in notations relating to all the parts required to make the building an engineering success.

We discovered a multitude of graffiti on the walls of the granary in the main barns. This has been catalogued and can be accessed online just Google Cragend Farm graffiti.

When restoring the Silo the joiners said that the top stairs were still fit for purpose and having cleaned them they were replaced.

The archaeologists also found graffiti on the Silo stairs.

Names on the Silo stairs

Five names are legible amongst the graffiti. Of the five, three are accompanied by place names, and one is not entirely legible. The names, and possible information regarding that person are as follows:

- William Last, Longframlington
- It is possible that this William Last is the same as is listed on the 1891 census for Northumberland as the nephew of Henry Last. William Last was born in 1857 in Belsay and his profession is listed as labourer.
- R Maxwel [sic] Rothbury
  It was not possible to find any information regarding this person.
- Bil Ball(e)(i)ntyne Rothbury
  A William Ballentyne is registered as being born in Elsdon in 1853 and his occupation during the 1881 census is listed as
- an Agricultural Labourer. In 1901, the same William Ballentyne is listed as living at Addycombe Cottages in Rothbury, working as a carter on a farm.
- Jane Todd
  Jane Todd was born in Rothbury in 1871 to James and Margaret Todd. At the time of the 1901 Northumberland census,
  The Todd family are all living at Cragend where her father (James Todd) , is listed as employed as Cragend Farm Steward and Jane is listed as an outworker.

History coming alive:

It was during open discussion at the end of a tour that the one of the guests commented that the reason they had come along was that a member of their family was known to have stayed at Cragend Farm in the early 20th century.

We were told that their name was "Blenkinsopp" a good Peak District name, but an unusual Northumberland name.

At this point we were unsure how we were going to prove that this family may have stayed at Cragend, until we looked at the Cragend Graffiti Report that was done by archaeologists in 2012 as part of a wider project to record the historic detail of the farm .

The graffiti, some 500 inscriptions, ranges from 1860's to the present day, and many are from the First and Second World War. Luckily for us the graffiti is catalogued on an Excel sheet which made it relatively simple for us to search for the name Blenkinsopp.

And there it was! 1903! Wow!
Building H   h1a   7   pencil on timber - handwriting
*   name weather date   1903   John Ble/Robert Dunn (underlined)/Andrew Gunvey (underlined)/John Bell (underlined)/John Blenkinsopp (underlined)/Sept 2nd 1903/a very wet day*

This gentleman was the grandfather of our visitor and went on to be cattle judge in the Peak District in later life.

It appears that Mr J Blenkinsopp and his family of wife with five children travelled from the Peak District (Chatsworth/Bakewell) to Cragside as a cattle handler.

As we know, Lord Armstrong had built the farm to house his prize cattle and so it came as no surprise that a worker from another county may have been here looking for the job or that perhaps the worker had heard that a cattle handler was required in this prestigious Northumberland Estate.

It is possible that Mr Blenkinsopp was here at the farm to work in 1903 with the cattle and either drive them elsewhere or sell them on behalf of the new Lord Armstrong who did not have an interest in the cattle.

It has been so exciting to find a living relative of the graffiti writers, especially one who was not from our local area and it has been thanks to the Heritage Open Days that this has come to light.
As we have found new information about the Silo building we have been able to edit the Historic England listing to an earlier date from 1895 to 1884.

Chapter 22

Importance of the whole site

None of the machinery will ever work again because the Blackburn Lake is now drained (flooding in c1927) and although No 490 is not listed, and its importance must not be overlooked.

It was the power for many different machines that operated in the barns, all run from drive shafts, fly wheels and belts.

It is also the main On/Off tap for the Silo building, which is powered curiously from the south side of the building, and until our excavations, it was unknown where the water entered the building.

It has since been excavated and using metal detectors we have found all the pipework.

See youtube video Minecraft pipework. Cragend Farm

Chapter 23

The Custodian Prize Historic Houses 2023

When we found the technical drawing we were able to raise our heads high and be proud of the work we are doing here at Cragend Farm.

The judges are amongst many who feel that this farm is of huge importance to our heritage and history.

The award will hopefully raise our profile and we can tell this tale of not just an ancient farm, but a Northumbrian farm, that became a Victorian Demonstration Centre for Agriculture and Industry using natural resources.

Winston Churchill said, "Those that fail to learn from history are doomed to repeat it."

Armstrong may not be everyone's cup of tea, certainly his sales of armaments leave a bitter taste for many, however his realisation that science was moving apace and needed to be carefully controlled before resources ran out was spot on.

Mary Beard recently gave a lecture on 'Who owns the past?' which is well worth a listen. It really sums up what we are trying to achieve here at Cragend Farm.

She states: 'Not discussing and displaying artifacts from the past is a glaring irony of "hiding the complexities of history and our own entanglement in it"... and that "this country has a nasty and inglorious record of carefully keeping its exploitation out of sight." She goes on to recommend that this is remedied with tactile and sensory access to historic sites that are not dummed down.
Our tours aim to be just that.

The Collection comprises of many items found at Cragend Farm including the large machinery and also older items including roundshot and maps, and below is just a small selection of coins and medals dating through the ages.

1. Silver sixpence Young Victoria 1842-1862 dates to be confirmed [1—2] hole in date. Hair with ribbons. Reeded.
2. George II 1739 Half penny
3. Cartwheel coin 1797
4. 1806 George III half penny
5. Northumberland fusiliers badge clip 1880's
6. Queen Victoria 60th Jubilee anniversary Commemorative badge 1897
7. Queen Victoria 1862 Bunn head Half penny
8. George III half penny
9. Royal Visit to Newcastle Commemorative Medal? 1884 Prince and Princess of Wales.
10. Thaler c1500, Hungarian dinar c1300,
11. William III coin c1690,
12. silver farthing cut quarter c1200,
13. Queen Victoria Golden Jubilee Medal 1897
14. Prince & Princess of Wales Visit to Newcastle Commemorative Coin 1884

Further reading -   Extra information:

[32] *https://doi.org/10.1680/jdare.21.00002*
Dams and Cragside 2021 Benn, J. 2021 .Lord Armstrong and the lakes
of Cragside, Northumberland. Paper 2100002

Table 1. Summary details of the lakes on Lord Armstrong's Coquetdale estates

Name	Date of construction	Catchment area: km²	Volume: m³	Lake TWL: mAODN
Tumbleton Lake NU 0691 0266	1866	12.2 (direct) 1.8 (indirect)	100 000	110
Debdon Lake NU 0650 0280	1870	11.0 (direct)	58 000	121
Nelly's Moss North NU 0803 0234	1885	0.2 (direct) 2.8 (indirect)	50 000	190
Nelly's Moss South NU 0789 0193	1885	0.4 (direct) 2.8 (indirect)	109 000	177
Blackburn Lake NU 0878 0194	c.1870	7.8 (direct)	150 000	153
Trewhitt Lake NT 9912 0462	1884	8.5 (direct)	85 000	115

Table 2. Summary details of the dams on Lord Armstrong's Coquetdale estates

Name	Dam type	Dam length: m	Dam height: m
Tumbleton Lake	Earth embankment	250	11.0
Debdon Lake	Earth embankment	260	5.0
Nelly's Moss North	South: earth embankment	125	3.0
	North: earth embankment	100	4.5
	East: masonry	175	1.5
Nelly's Moss South	South: earth embankment	95	4.0
	East: earth embankment	220	3.0
Blackburn Lake	South west: earth embankment	155	4.0
	South east: earth embankment	200	4.0
Trewhitt Lake	Earth embankment	165	5.0

116

Chapter 24

The book 'The Magician of the North' is about Lord Armstrong of Cragside . This biography mentions Cragend Farm as one of the Estate Farms. When Henrietta Heald, the biographer, came on a Cragend Farm tour she had no idea of what amazing hydraulics were hidden here.

She has also written the National Trust Cragside brochure.

Cragside had plans for the farm back in 1988 which never came to fruition. NT Cragside continue to be a source of information.

Taken from her book about Armstrong Page 130:

"Tumbleton lake was formed by damming the Debden burn lower down creating a head of water to serve the pumphouse of 1866 were pumps driven by a hydraulic engine provided water to Cragside House. Meanwhile the main course of Blackburn was dammed to form the largest of the five lakes which was used for the boating and fishing as well as the provision of hydraulic power to Cragend Farm."

Dates from the Thomas Sopwith diaries at The Robinson Library, Newcastle University talk about boating, which was on Tumbleton Lake in 1866, but The Thatched Boathouse at Blackburn Lake shows that boating was also enjoyed there.

Further text once again listing Cragend Farm, machinery and the cattle can be found in the 1885 A Guide to Rothbury and surrounding district by A. E. Scott

'Passing about 1 mile east from the Reivers Well we come to Cragend one of Sir Williams farms where some fine stock may be seen including several of the famous breed called wild Duchess of Geneva from Teeside. Here also may be seeing some wonderful machines driven by water power for crushing corn, threshing, ploughing et cetera. The water is supplied from the lake.'

Chapter 25

Magazine article about Cragend in Northern Mills Magazine

Cragend – A peculiar turbine
Tom Hay writes about an odd turbine at Cragend Farm. This article is compiled from two by Tom.

"I have been going through my collection of 1960s mill photographs and am very puzzled by the turbine which drove a chaff cutter at Cragend Farm (NU086009) on the Cragside Estate at Rothbury.

At the time I just thought that it was a vortex turbine without guide vanes but now realise it is something completely unlike any turbine I have seen anywhere.

It looks as though it is an impulse type with an angled top entry, and with the water discharge out of the rectangular base. There is a pulley belt drive on the far side with a very thick belt coiled up on the floor behind the inlet pipe.

I wondered if it could be one of Armstrong's brain waves made at Elswick.

I struggled to get additional information on the turbine so I went to the Tyne and Wear archives and found, to my delight, in the Armstrong Family Papers catalogue (Accession No DF/A) correspondence between Gilkes of Kendal and Armstrong at Cragside. The letters, written in 1884 concern the mystery turbine.

In the February letter there is a reference to a 30hp turbine (which would be Gilkes No 490, a 10" inlet and twin 7" outlet vortex type operating under 190 ft head) which was still there in the 1960s and drove a threshing machine and other equipment.

The March letter refers to a turbine to drive a "chaff cutter" to chop green forage to make silage and Gilkes strongly recommends their "tangent turbine" with an adjusting nozzle rather than their "reaction" wheel.

Then *"eureka"*, in the July letter about the tangent turbine for Cragend is a sketch of the machine which I photographed in the 1960s but could not identify.

So it is a Gilkes and could be their no. 630 rated at 4hp with a 4" inlet and unspecified outlet, under 200ft head. This head matches the Cragend site and the turbine water outlet is the rectangular opening in the base. The 4" inlet could refer to the size of nozzle used to give 3 hp as the inlet pipe, from memory, was bigger than 4".

However the turbine is not an "Armstrong Special" but what the internal nozzle and bucket arrangement is I cannot work out, since Pelton wheel turbines which Gilkes started making in 1884, have the inlet pipe and nozzle under the wheel and not tangential at about 45° over the top of the wheel.

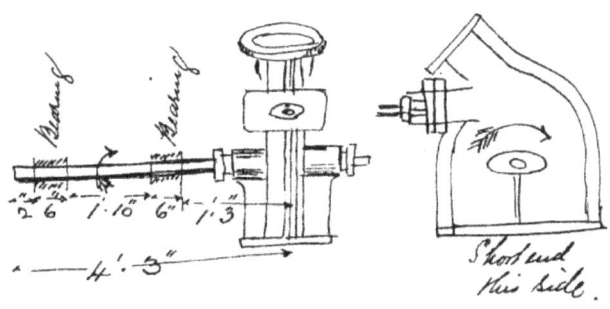

I cannot think it is a precursor to the Turgo Impulse turbine which Gilkes patented and first appeared in their 1922 catalogue as it has the inlet pipe and nozzle under the wheel and has a thrust bearing to locate the shaft as the jet strikes the wheel at the side.

At least we now know the name of this type of turbine and who made it and I wonder if any others have survived – the design may have been short lived as no-one seems to have seen it in any Gilkes catalogue.'

(written by Tom Hay)

Chapter 26

The Gilkes Turbines

Gilkes have been supplying hydro turbine products to the global market from as far back as 1856, since then we have delivered more than 6800 units to over 85 countries. Their world-renowned hydroelectric turbines now comprise Francis, Pelton and Turgo turbines (invented by Gilkes in 1919). They are capable of generating up to 30MW from a single unit and also include compact solutions for the 50kW to 100kW market.Every Gilkes Turbine is designed and optimised to provide the best annual energy production figures.

Gilkes Curator Historian Chris Crewdson correspondence in 2023:

Dear Lou
Thanks for your email.
I attach the pics of the Gilbert Gilkes & Co order ledger. The company was renamed ca 1928 when the business of James Gordon was acquired so we are now Gilbert Gilkes & Gordon Ltd.

The two turbines would have been made at Canal Iron Works, Kendal which is where they are still located today [though much modernised!]

The two machines were both in the Gilkes era so after 1881 [# 440 was the first machine made after Gilbert Gilkes bought the business]

Sadly, we have no records of prices paid [or at least that I have been able to find in the archive. Suffice it say that when Gilbert Gilkes bought to business from the Williamson Brothers in 1881 the stock, which would have included a few turbines, was values at £2,816 [about £347,000] today. Many of the turbines were sold for less than £100 in the 1880's.

The fact that the valves were made in Newcastle is entirely logical as Lord Armstrong's engineering works [from which he made his fortune

*] was in Newcastle and he may have chosen a Newcastle valve
manufacturer for both jobs.*

The turbines would definitely have been made in Kendal

Both machines are of the "Vortex "design.

*Turbine 490 was supplied to Sir W G Armstrong [of Cragside]
presumably for one of his farms at the time.
This machine was rated at 30hp on 190 ft head
I would guess this machine as ca 1882*

*Turbine 630 was also supplied to Lord Armstrong [by this time a Peer]
This machine was rated at 3hp on 200 ft so presumably using the
same water supply.
This machine was ordered around 1887?*

The headings are from left to right
No = serial number
HP = horsepower
F = Fall ... the head of water coming into the turbine.
Name = client or sometimes the factor/agent of an estate
Position = vertically [V] or horizontally [H] arrangement
Blades = Mov indicates movable guide vanes Fixed indicated fixed
guide vanes [most were movable]
Q = volumetric flow rate . The flow rate units are volume per unit
time. The standard metric unit is meter square per seconds m 3 / s .
No 490 Gilkes record. (now measured as cubic metres per second or
GPM gallons per minute. 112 Q/gpm)

Interestingly, on the Gilkes records for the No 630 the Q reference is
blank. The water used to power this low HP turbine is the exhaust
water from the hoist.

Supply = Diameter of supply [inlet pipe]
Suction = diameter of outlet pipe... referred to as suction because the
"draft tube" below a turbine creates suction and effectively increases

the operating head which is a combination of the fall plus the suction of the draft tube.

As Armstrong bought 490 and 491 at the same time I wondered where the other one is located. Unfortunately, our early records only rarely record the location of the turbine. (No 491 located at Trewitt Farm).

The #630 has something like 'new' and some gaps so perhaps it was truly experimental. It is certainly not fixed in the same manner as the 490. I think the word "new" will mean that a new pattern was made specifically for this job. This is probably because the turbine was designed for an output of 3hp as opposed to #490 which was designed for 30 hp.

The oldest turbine machine in operation and generating electricity is in Ireland at Dripsey Woollen Mill # 512 so this was in the Gilkes era.

The Pattern Type.

"Patterns" are the wooden models used to create the sand moulds into which the molten cast iron is poured.

Patterns can be used repeatedly to make castings so very often patterns would be used for different clients.

In the early days of the business the patterns would have been given names of clients eg Horsfells. This suggests #490 = Hobby #630= New.

An exhibition pattern would have been one made for an exhibit at a trade fair.

Note: National Trust Cragside hold records of Gilkes orders that comfirm dates of orders.

Chapter 27 War Time recollections

Milky Recollections of Cragend Farm from Anthea Logan-Wood
February 2024

This chapter is about the milking parlours in circa 1946 but also ties in with the floods and the reservoir damage.

Anthea was born in 1939 so she thinks these recollections are from when she was about 6-7 years old. Betty Thompson, who was 2 years older than her, (the daughter of George and Ada, and was later married to a Livingstone at Suers Hill), was a great friend of hers during this time and we have a photograph of them together.

Anthea and Betty 1944 and 1946 Cragend Farm

The west and middle bays were used for milking, and the cattle were led in from the west door. The top room (now our dining room described as a two legged table) also held cattle.

They were tethered up to the walls, with a ball of hay to eat whilst they were being milked. At that point there were no fixed stalls but the floors were of stone with gullys for cleaning them. This was a 365 days a year job.

They were milked by hand into a bucket by George Senior, Ada his wife and Jimmy Thompson. Eldest son George Jnr went to war in the RAF and died in action in 1945.

The buckets were taken to the Cooling Room to the north of the parlour and placed in a cooling bath, whereby water was flowing from pipes, taken off the spring water on the hill, and drained out into The Coquet below through drains.

Anthea was allowed to have a go at milking. Sitting on a stool you leaned into the rear/flank of the cow and place your hands on their udders with the bucket underneath.

There were a number of farm cats (mainly feral) who would line up to have a saucer of milk there, and sometimes, Jimmy would squirt them direct from the cows udders.

It is unclear what breed they were, 'mottled' could mean Blue-Greys (a cross between Whitebred Shorthorn and a Galloway) but possibly Beef Shorthorns which can be also red and roan. She thinks there would have been about 8 in each parlour, so approx. 18+ cows. The bull resided in the Bull Pen.

She has recollection of a machine in the Cooling Room which may have been a cream separator (cream/milk Alfa Laval). Everything was rationed during the war with cream being particularly expensive.

The buckets of milk were bottled to take on a milk round and the remaining milk was placed in churns. Anthea remembers the bottles were wide necked and had cardboard bottle tops. These tops sat inside the top of the bottle that had a wide neck to accommodate them. The children would a press out a hole in them, and use them for making pom-poms/bobbles for hats. These were lifted by a sack-barrow, to be taken by a milk lorry, that collected them at the road end, set on a platform ready for collection. It is unclear where the milk churns went to, but Rothbury seems likely, with Longframlington and Longhorsley being further away and possibly having their own dairies nearby.

George Snr had his own milk round locally.

There was a cloudburst(flood) in [12th] August 1946, and all the roads in and out of Rothbury were closed off due to water, mud and debris for many days.

George Snr had a van with a canvas back for his milk round, and the crates of milk went in the back of this van. Anthea's mother and aunt, (who were living at the Cragside Cragend Cottages during the war), followed behind the van and Anthea was in the back with the bottles of milk, clanking around, all went to Rothbury to get some provisions/food.

At this time, The Armstrong's were not residing at Cragside as the military were using it during WWII. They drove up, through Cragend top field, to the carriage drive, and on up past [the lakes] The Kennels, onto the Alnwick Road to avoid all the blocked roads; and onto Hillside to drop down into Rothbury (at closest it is the nearest village 2 miles+ away) by Phillips Newsagents. The road into Rothbury was in a terrible state because The Coplish Burn, Rothbury, had flooded and all the water and mud, had gone all over the road at Townfoot in Rothbury. Anthea, and her mother and aunt were lifted over the mud by George so that they could get to the shops in Rothbury for food.

The Italian POWs were helping to clear the roads and were shovelling all the mud and debris away from the newsagents at Townfoot.

The Blackburn had been drained and she remembers there being no water in it by this time.

Previously, The Blackburn Lake had burst its dam and was drained having dumped large piles of debris at its base where it meets The Coquet. (No date but we think c1928).

Reference:
https://www.gov.uk/flood-and-coastal-erosion-risk-management-research-reports/lessons-learnt-from-historical-dam-incidents

[72] Tumbleton Lake Incident date: 12 August 1946
Construction details The 11-m high embankment was constructed in 1885 near
Rothbury, Northumberland.

Incident description Torrential rain swept across Northumberland on 12 August 1946.
The dam was overtopped and came close to failure. The spillway channel was destroyed and a bridge over it was severely damaged. The downstream face was scoured. The dam had been overtopped to a lesser extent on 21 July 1927.

Response The structure was so impaired that it was kept empty for many years.
Lessons This small dam had an undersized spillway.
Reference: Archer, 1992.

Some Milk Bottle Chronology which emphasises how farming practices occurred in terms of technology:

- 1880 – British milk bottles were first produced by the Express Dairy Company, these were delivered by horse-drawn carts. The first bottles used a porcelain stopper top held on by wire. Lewis Whiteman patents the glass milk bottle with a glass lid.
- 1884 – Dr. Thatcher invents the glass milk container in New York. These were initially sealed with wooden plugs, which proved unsuccessful, and were soon replaced by glass stoppers.[8]
- 1894 – Anthony Hailwood developed the milk pasteurisation process to create sterilized milk, which could be safely stored for longer periods.
- 1920 – Advertisements began to appear on milk bottles. A sand-blasting technique was used to etch them on the glass.
- 1930s – Increased prevalence of battery electric vehicles as milk floats[9]
- mid-1950s – Paperboard tops were deemed unhygienic and banned in some locations. Delivery by horse-drawn carts was still common.[citation needed]
- early-1990s – The advertising largely disappeared with the introduction of infrared bottle scanners designed to check cleanliness.

Chapter 28

The Renwick's have added to the history of the Armstrong legacy by transforming the Turbine Room into a historical site for future generations to appreciate.

The slate roof, floors and stairs of the Silo and some stonework have been repaired.

My special thanks to Shaun, who made the mad decision to buy this farm, after quite a few sleepless nights of wondering if it was the right thing to do, and one sleepless night where we both tested it out on site in sleeping bags just to be sure.

The Silo Turbine No 630, and Silo Hoist No 1306 and the vital Turbine Room No 490 are being preserved for future generations.

Acknowledgments

My thanks to Paul Stott, Bridget Gubbins, and Michael Chaplin who made me believe I could write this, and to all my family and friends for supporting me whilst compiling this book.

There is a long list of people, they know who they are but here are some of the main players who have helped with research and our journey here at Cragend Farm:

Chris Crewdson – Gilkes, Kendal
John Allan, National Trust Engineer Cragside
Anthea Logan-Wood – evacuee during WWII to Cragend Farm
Northumberland Estates Archives, Alnwick Castle.
Historic Houses
Roger Kagan – weighbridge restoration
Hannah Aspey - Guru regarding brand and content development
Margaret Straughan -resident at West Cottage
Peter McKenzie – ex Vickers Armstrong curator
George Thompson – tenant farmer Cragend farm until 2009
National Library of Scotland
Tyne & Wear Archives
British Newspaper Archives
Roger Kagan
David Humble
Storey & Edmondson
Ancestry.com
Historic Houses
Leo and Alice Dugdale
Penny Ford
Anna McGowan
Annie Lloyd
Stephen Teather
Jonny, Peter and Paul (The Detectorists)
Matt Baker and the Big Circus team
Visit Northumberland Partnership
Deccy Horton (nee Thompson)
Pauline Robison

Sharon Wetherby
Dr Chris Scott and Dr Gillian Scott
Seb Littlewood (Beamish)
Eileen Telfer (great grand-daughter of Silo Worker Joseph Gall).
David Jones
Rothbury History Society
Coquetdale Geological Society
Susan Barwood
Susan Aynsley
Fabulous North
Rothbury History Society
The Northumbrian Magazine
Vintage Spirit Magazine
Build It Magazine
Dave Burton and Heather Dixon

and everyone else who has helped along the way – Thank you!

Lou Renwick lives at Cragend Farm with her family and two Border Collies, Rare Breed animals and lots of trees and bees.

www.cragendfarm.co.uk

Our Cragend Farm Historic Story to 2024

View of Cragend Farm from the Cragside Carriage Drive

Cragend Photos Credit Dave Burton Photography

THE END

www.ingramcontent.com/pod-product-compliance
Ingram Content Group UK Ltd.
Pitfield, Milton Keynes, MK11 3LW, UK
UKHW041353280125
4330UKWH00040B/887